Mama's *Italian* Cookbook

Just like Mama used to make

This edition published in 2010
LOVE FOOD is an imprint of Parragon Books Ltd

Parragon
Queen Street House
4 Queen Street
Bath BA1 1HE, UK

ISBN: 978-1-4075-7958-0

Printed in China

Internal design by Sabine Vonderstein
Mama's world created by Dominic Utton
Project managed by Faye Lloyd

Mama and all characters mentioned in this book are entirely fictitious. Any similarity to any person,
living or dead, is purely co-incidental and unintended.

Notes for the Reader
This book uses imperial, metric, and US cup measurements. Follow the same units of measurement
throughout; do not mix imperial and metric. All spoon measurements are level: teaspoons are assumed to
be 5 ml, and tablespoons are assumed to be 15 ml. Unless otherwise stated, milk is assumed to be whole,
eggs and individual vegetables such as potatoes are medium, and pepper is freshly ground black pepper.

The times given are an approximate guide only. Preparation times differ according to the techniques used
by different people and the cooking times may also vary from those given as a result of the type of oven
used. Optional ingredients, variations, or serving suggestions have not been included in the calculations.

Recipes using raw or very lightly cooked eggs should be avoided by infants, the elderly, pregnant women,
convalescents, and anyone with a chronic condition. Pregnant and breast-feeding women are advised
to avoid eating peanuts and peanut products. People with nut allergies should be aware that some of
the prepared ingredients used in the recipes in this book may contain nuts. Always check the packaging
before use.

Contents

Introduction

Welcome to Mama's Italian Cookbook — not only a collection of recipes from my own kitchen, but a scrapbook of family wisdom and a little insight into my life. For me, there is no distinction between the cooking and the cook: the feelings, the passion, the love, and the experiences of the person making the food all go into the food — and so the cook becomes a part of the recipe. All of which means, to understand my food is to understand me.

So let me tell you about myself. People call me Mama. I'm the head of a large, noisy, happy household here in a small village in Apulia, a region in the south of Italy. I've been married to Alberto for 56 years and together we have 6 children, 22 grandchildren, and 8 great-grandchildren. I've lived in this village all of my life — and my mama, her mama, and her mama before her, all did the same. Tradition is everything here.

And nowhere is tradition more clearly seen than in the kitchen. Learning how to feed a family is a skill and a passion that is passed down the generations; and it is a source of pride with me that, even in the hardest times, I have always put beautiful, healthy food on my table — and my family have grown strong and beautiful themselves as a result.

Good food needn't be complicated: simple dishes put together with care and love can be the match of the most decorated chefs in the ristoranti of Roma and Milano. In Mama's kitchen we have just one test: if four generations of the same family can sit down and enjoy a meal together, if every plate is wiped clean and every stomach satisfied, then Mama's done her job well.

Of course, I may be the head of a family over 36 strong (and I don't include myself or Alberto in that, nor our many cousins, nephews, nieces — all of whom can often be found sitting at our table or harassing

9

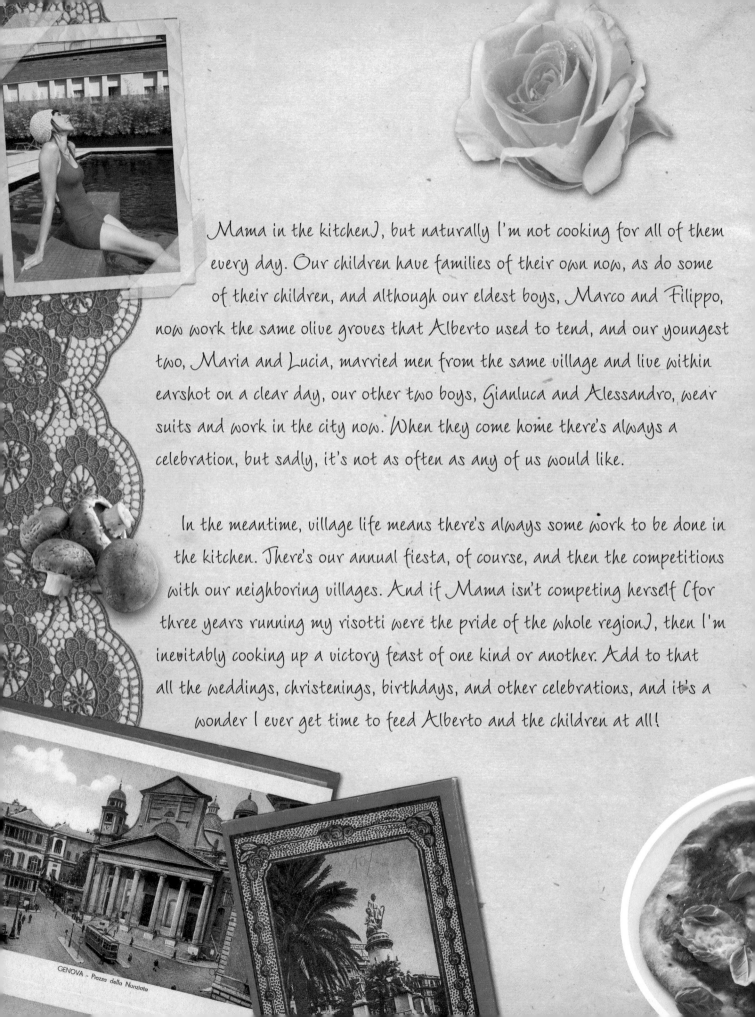

Mama in the kitchen), but naturally I'm not cooking for all of them every day. Our children have families of their own now, as do some of their children, and although our eldest boys, Marco and Filippo, now work the same olive groves that Alberto used to tend, and our youngest two, Maria and Lucia, married men from the same village and live within earshot on a clear day, our other two boys, Gianluca and Alessandro, wear suits and work in the city now. When they come home there's always a celebration, but sadly, it's not as often as any of us would like.

In the meantime, village life means there's always some work to be done in the kitchen. There's our annual fiesta, of course, and then the competitions with our neighboring villages. And if Mama isn't competing herself (for three years running my risotti were the pride of the whole region), then I'm inevitably cooking up a victory feast of one kind or another. Add to that all the weddings, christenings, birthdays, and other celebrations, and it's a wonder I ever get time to feed Alberto and the children at all!

All of my experience has gone into this book —
and all the experience of those who taught me:
my Mama and her Mama before her. It is not
simply a collection of recipes, it's an expression of
who I am.

Most cookbooks are written like textbooks — reading them is like listening
to cooking teachers. This one's different. This is Mama's cookbook. And we
have a saying in Apulia: "Una buona mamma vale cento maestre" (a good
mother is worth a hundred teachers).

Buon appetito!

Mama's Simple Suppers

All good cooking starts with simplicity. Get the basics — the principi fondamentali — right and all else will follow. Before you can tackle the big parties and the showcase dishes, you have to learn how to make simple suppers. These are the recipes Mama learned as a little girl, standing on tiptoe in the kitchen, watching her Mama — and they are still the staple of our household mealtimes.

What could be more heartwarming than homemade Tuscan bean soup? What could be more wholesome than spaghetti with meatballs? And what better way to finish any meal than with Mama's chocolate and nut cake?

These are the tastes of authentic Italian cooking.
Enjoy!

Minestrone
Hearty vegetable and pasta soup

serves 4

2 tbsp olive oil
2 garlic cloves, chopped
2 red onions, chopped
2¾ oz/75 g prosciutto, sliced
1 red bell pepper,
    seeded and chopped
1 orange bell pepper,
    seeded and chopped
14 oz/400 g canned chopped
    tomatoes
4 cups vegetable stock
1 celery stalk, trimmed and
    sliced
1½ cups canned cranberry
    beans, drained and rinsed
1 cup shredded green leafy
    cabbage
2/3 cup frozen peas, thawed
1 tbsp chopped fresh parsley
2¾ oz/75 g dried vermicelli pasta
salt and pepper
freshly grated Parmesan cheese,
    to garnish
fresh crusty bread, to serve

Heat the oil in a large saucepan. Add the garlic, onions, and prosciutto and cook over medium heat, stirring, for 3 minutes, until slightly softened. Add the bell peppers and the chopped tomatoes and cook for an additional 2 minutes, stirring. Stir in the stock, then add the celery, beans, cabbage, peas, and parsley. Season with salt and pepper.

Bring to a boil, then reduce the heat and simmer for 30 minutes.

Add the pasta to the pan. Cook for an additional 10—12 minutes, or according to the package instructions. Remove from the heat and ladle into warmed bowls. Garnish with some freshly grated Parmesan cheese and serve with fresh crusty bread.

Pappa al pomodoro
Bread and tomato soup

Chop the bread into rough chunks, about 1 inch/2.5 cm square. Place a heavy-bottom saucepan over medium heat. Add the stock, oil, and sage and simmer until reduced by half. Add the bread and garlic, increase the heat to high, and fry until all the liquid has been soaked up and the bread begins to become crispy.

Add the tomatoes and sugar, stir, and simmer for 15 minutes. Add hot water to thin the soup to your preferred consistency (it should be thick). Simmer for an additional minute. Season with salt and pepper.

Ladle into warmed bowls, sprinkle a little Parmesan cheese on top, and serve.

serves 6

10½ oz/300 g sourdough bread
generous ½ cup chicken stock
4 tbsp extra virgin olive oil
3 tbsp shredded fresh sage leaves
4 garlic cloves, peeled and
    finely chopped
1 lb 12 oz/800 g canned peeled
    plum tomatoes
1 tsp sugar
1 cup hot water
salt and pepper
½ cup grated Parmesan cheese,
    to garnish

Ribollita
Tuscan bean soup

serves 6

2 cups canned cannellini beans,
   drained and rinsed
2 cups canned cranberry beans,
   drained and rinsed
2½ cups vegetable stock
4 oz/115 g dried conchigliette
   or other small pasta shapes
4 tbsp olive oil
2 garlic cloves, finely chopped
3 tbsp chopped fresh flat-leaf
   parsley
salt and pepper

Place half the cannellini beans and half the cranberry beans in a food processor with half the stock and process until smooth. Pour into a large, heavy-bottom saucepan and add the remaining beans. Stir in enough of the remaining stock to achieve the consistency you like, then bring to a boil. Add the pasta and return to a boil, then reduce the heat and cook for 15 minutes, or until just tender.

Meanwhile, heat 3 tablespoons of the oil in a small skillet. Add the garlic and cook, stirring continuously, for 2—3 minutes, or until golden. Stir the garlic into the soup with the parsley.

Season with salt and pepper and ladle into warmed bowls. Drizzle with the remaining olive oil and serve immediately.

Mama's tips for running a smooth household

Organization is the key to an easy life — in the kitchen and out of it. Alberto knew every leaf on every branch in the olive groves, and I could cook blindfolded here if I had to. Keep your kitchen tidy and clean, and half your work is done already.

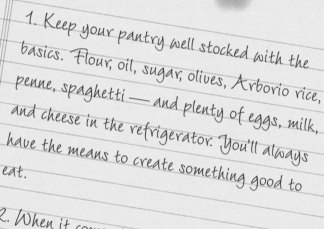

1. Keep your pantry well stocked with the basics. Flour, oil, sugar, olives, Arborio rice, penne, spaghetti — and plenty of eggs, milk, and cheese in the refrigerator. You'll always have the means to create something good to eat.

2. When it comes to olive oil, buy the best you can afford. A cheap oil can ruin good cooking.

3. Plan your meals for the week. Taking 15 minutes every Sunday night to organize yourself will save money, save time, and save throwing food away needlessly.

Herbs are the difference between a dish tasting okay and tasting eccellente. A sprinkle of the right leaves can take a dish into the sublime, and every kitchen windowsill should have a row of pots: basil, rosemary, and oregano at the very least. They're easy to grow, they bring a bit of the garden into the house, and they save Mama trailing outside all the time.

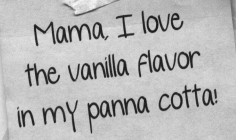

Mama, I love the vanilla flavor in my panna cotta!

Grow what you can. Fresh insalata made from lettuce, arugula, spinach, and tomatoes costs nothing—and tastes like pure Italian sunshine.

Take control. Roma had only one emperor: and so must your household. There's no democracy in the kitchen: Mama's in charge and that's final.

Manage your time: You only have one pair of hands, one pair of legs, and one pair of eyes. My son Alessandro talks about something called "multitasking" — it sounds like making life unnecessarily complicated to me. My Mama didn't multitask, and neither did her Mama. Do one thing at a time, and do it well.

Insalata di fagioli bicolore
Green and white bean salad

serves 4

½ cup dried cannellini beans
beans, soaked overnight
8 oz/225 g fine green beans,
trimmed
¼ red onion, thinly sliced
12 black olives, pitted
1 tbsp chopped chives

dressing
½ tbsp lemon juice
½ tsp Dijon mustard
6 tbsp extra virgin olive oil
salt and pepper

Drain the soaked beans and put in a saucepan with plenty of fresh water to cover. Bring to a boil, then boil rapidly for 15 minutes. Reduce the heat slightly and cook for an additional 30 minutes, or until tender but not disintegrating. Add salt in the last 5 minutes of cooking. Drain and set aside.

Meanwhile, bring a large saucepan of water to a boil, plunge the green beans into the water, return to a boil, and cook for 4 minutes, until just tender but still brightly colored and crunchy. Drain and set aside. Whisk together the dressing ingredients, then let stand.

While both types of beans are still slightly warm, tip them into a shallow serving dish or arrange on individual warmed plates. Scatter over the onion slices, olives, and chives. Whisk the dressing again and spoon over the salad.

Serve immediately at room temperature.

Olio e sale alla Barese
Tomato salad with cucumber

serves 4

1 small cucumber, peeled
2 beefsteak tomatoes
1 onion
4 tbsp olive oil
2 tbsp white wine vinegar
2 slices of white country bread
salt and pepper

Thinly slice the cucumber and tomatoes and place them in a salad bowl. Slice the onion into fine rings, then toss them with the cucumber and tomatoes.

Whisk together the olive oil and vinegar, season with salt and pepper, and pour over the salad. Marinate for 20 minutes.

Toast the bread slices on both sides under a broiler or in the oven until golden brown, then cut into bite-size pieces. Toss them into the salad and serve immediately.

Insalata di pollo
Braised chicken salad

serves 4

3 tbsp olive oil
1 chicken, about 3 lb/1.3 kg
1 cup dry white wine
1 onion, chopped
1 carrot, chopped
1 celery stalk, chopped
1 fresh bay leaf
salt and pepper

Preheat the oven to 350°F/180°C. Heat the olive oil in an ovenproof casserole over medium—high heat. Add the chicken and fry for 15 minutes, turning, until golden all over. Pour in the wine and simmer for 2 minutes, then add the onion, carrot, celery, and bay leaf. Season with salt and pepper. Cover tightly and transfer to the oven. Bake for 45—50 minutes, turning every 20 minutes, until the juices from the thickest part of the thigh run clear when pierced with a skewer. Discard the liquid and solids. When cool enough to handle, remove and discard the skin.

Strip the meat from the bone, slicing any large chunks into bite-size pieces.

Arrange the chicken in a dish. Sprinkle with the peppercorns and bay leaves and season with salt. Pour in enough oil to coat generously. Cover tightly with plastic wrap and marinate in the refrigerator for 1—2 days.

Remove the chicken from the refrigerator 2 hours before serving. Place in a colander set over a bowl to drain, and let stand until the oil has liquefied.

serves 4

marinade
1 tsp black peppercorns
4 fresh bay leaves
½ cup olive oil
salt

salad
5 cups baby spinach
   leaves
1 head chicory
5 tender celery stalks
1 tsp wine vinegar
1 tsp balsamic vinegar
salt

To make the salad, chop the leaves as desired. Combine the spinach, chicory, and celery in a large serving dish. Toss with salt, enough oil from the chicken to just coat the leaves, and the wine vinegar. Arrange the chicken on top, discarding the peppercorns and bay leaves. Sprinkle with the balsamic vinegar before serving.

Insalata di prosciutto, salami e fichi
Ham and salami salad with figs

serves 6

9-12 ripe figs, depending on size
6 thin slices dry-cured
    Italian ham
12 thin slices salami
1 small bunch fresh basil,
    separated into small sprigs
few fresh mint sprigs
1 small bunch arugula
2 tbsp freshly squeezed
    lemon juice
4 tbsp extra virgin olive oil
salt and pepper

Trim the stems of the figs to leave just a short length, then cut the figs into quarters.

Arrange the ham and salami on a large serving platter. Wash and dry the herbs and arugula and put in a bowl with the prepared figs.

Whisk together the lemon juice and oil with a fork in a small bowl and season well with salt and pepper.

Pour the dressing over the herbs and arugula and carefully turn the figs and greens until they are well coated.

Spoon the figs and greens onto the meat and arrange around the platter.

Antipasti misti di carne
Mixed antipasto meat platter

Italian Prosciutto di Parma

serves 4

1 cantaloupe melon
2 oz/55 g Italian salami,
   thinly sliced
8 slices prosciutto
8 slices bresaola
8 slices mortadella
4 plum tomatoes, thinly sliced
4 fresh figs, quartered
2/3 cup black olives, pitted
2 tbsp shredded fresh
   basil leaves
4 tbsp extra virgin olive oil,
   plus extra to serve
pepper
sliced ciabatta loaf, to serve

Cut the melon in half, scoop out and discard the seeds, then cut the flesh into 8 wedges. Arrange the wedges on one half of a large serving platter.

Arrange the salami, prosciutto, bresaola, and mortadella in loose folds on the other half of the platter. Arrange the tomato slices and fig quarters along the center of the platter.

Sprinkle the olives and shredded basil over the platter and drizzle with olive oil. Season with pepper, then serve with slices of ciabatta and extra olive oil for dipping and drizzling.

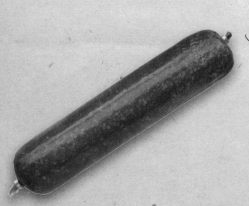

Salami Sausage

Black Olive

Bruschetta ai funghi selvatici
Wild mushroom bruschetta

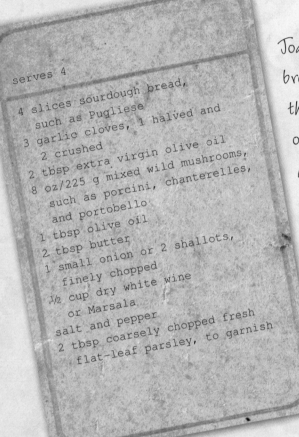

serves 4

4 slices sourdough bread,
    such as Pugliese
3 garlic cloves, 1 halved and
    2 crushed
2 tbsp extra virgin olive oil
8 oz/225 g mixed wild mushrooms,
    such as porcini, chanterelles,
    and portobello
1 tbsp olive oil
2 tbsp butter
1 small onion or 2 shallots,
    finely chopped
1/2 cup dry white wine
    or Marsala
salt and pepper
2 tbsp coarsely chopped fresh
    flat-leaf parsley, to garnish

Toast the bread slices on both sides under a preheated broiler or in a preheated, ridged grill pan, then rub with the garlic halves and drizzle with the extra virgin olive oil. Transfer to a cookie sheet and keep warm in a warm oven. Wipe the mushrooms thoroughly to remove any trace of soil, and slice any large ones. Heat the olive oil with half the butter in a skillet, then add the mushrooms and cook over medium heat, stirring frequently, for 3—4 minutes, or until softened. Remove with a slotted spoon and keep warm in the oven.

Heat the remaining butter in the skillet, add the onion and crushed garlic, then cook over medium heat, stirring frequently, for 3—4 minutes, or until softened. Add the wine and stir well, then let bubble for 2—3 minutes, or until reduced and thickened. Return the mushrooms to the skillet and heat through. The sauce should be thick enough to glaze the mushrooms.

Season with salt and pepper. Pile the mushrooms on top of the warm bruschetta, then garnish with parsley and serve immediately.

Funghi ripieni con spinaci e pancetta
Mushrooms stuffed with bacon and spinach

serves 4

5 cups fresh baby spinach leaves
4 portobello mushrooms
3 tbsp olive oil
2 oz/55 g rindless bacon,
  finely diced
2 garlic cloves, crushed
1 cup fresh white breadcrumbs or
  brown breadcrumbs
2 tbsp chopped fresh basil
salt and pepper

Preheat the oven to 400°F/200°C. Rinse the spinach and place in a saucepan with just the water clinging to the leaves. Cook for 2—3 minutes, until wilted. Drain, squeezing out as much liquid as possible, and finely chop. Cut the stalks from the mushrooms and finely chop, reserving the whole caps.

Heat 2 tablespoons of the oil in a skillet. Add the mushroom caps, round-side down, and cook for 1 minute. Remove from the skillet and arrange, round-side down, in a large ovenproof dish. Add the chopped mushroom stalks, bacon, and garlic to the skillet and cook for 5 minutes.

Stir in the spinach, breadcrumbs, and basil and season with salt and pepper. Mix well and divide the stuffing among the mushroom caps. Drizzle the remaining oil over the top. Bake in the preheated oven for 20 minutes, until crisp and golden.

Mama's Tip

Little dice of bacon with chopped spinach, garlic, and crisp, golden breadcrumbs make a delicious stuffing for oven-baked mushrooms. They can be served straight from the oven, or prepared ahead of time and served at room temperature.

Frittata di frutti di mare
Seafood omelet

serves 3

2 tbsp unsalted butter
1 tbsp olive oil
1 onion, finely chopped
1 small-medium zucchini, halved
   lengthwise and sliced
1 celery stalk, finely chopped
1½ cups button mushrooms, sliced
2 oz/55 g green beans, cut into
   2-inch/5-cm lengths
4 eggs
scant ½ cup mascarpone cheese
1 tbsp chopped fresh thyme
1 tbsp shredded fresh basil
7 oz/200 g canned tuna,
   drained and flaked
4 oz/115 g shelled cooked shrimp
salt and pepper

Preheat the broiler. Melt the butter with the olive oil in a heavy-bottom skillet with a flameproof handle. If the skillet has a wooden handle, protect it with foil because it needs to go under the broiler. Add the onion and cook over low heat, stirring occasionally, for 5 minutes, until softened.

Add the zucchini, celery, mushrooms, and beans and cook, stirring occasionally, for an additional 8–10 minutes, until starting to brown.

Beat the eggs with the mascarpone cheese, thyme, basil, and salt and pepper.

Add the tuna to the skillet and stir it into the mixture with a wooden spoon. Add the shrimp. Pour the egg mixture into the skillet and cook for 5 minutes, until it is just starting to set. Draw the egg from the sides of the skillet toward the center to let the uncooked egg run underneath.

Put the skillet under the preheated broiler and cook until the egg is just set and the surface is starting to brown. Cut the omelet into wedges and serve.

Spaghetti con le polpette
Spaghetti with meatballs

serves 6

1 potato, diced
14 oz/400 g ground beef
1 onion, finely chopped
1 egg
4 tbsp chopped fresh flat-leaf
    parsley
all-purpose flour, for dusting
5 tbsp virgin olive oil
1¾ cups strained tomatoes
2 tbsp tomato paste
14 oz/400 g dried spaghetti
salt and pepper
6 fresh basil leaves, shredded,
    and freshly grated Parmesan
    cheese, to garnish

Place the potato in a small saucepan, add cold water to cover and a pinch of salt, and bring to a boil. Cook for 10–15 minutes, until tender, then drain. Either mash thoroughly with a potato masher or fork or pass through a potato ricer.

Combine the potato, ground beef, onion, egg, and parsley in a bowl and season with salt and pepper. Spread out the flour on a plate. With dampened hands, shape the meat mixture into walnut-size balls and roll in the flour. Shake off any excess.

Heat the oil in a heavy-bottom skillet, add the meatballs, and cook over medium heat, stirring and turning frequently, for 8–10 minutes, until golden all over. Add the strained tomatoes and tomato paste and cook for an additional 10 minutes, until the sauce is reduced and thickened. Meanwhile, bring a large saucepan of lightly salted water to a boil. Add the spaghetti, bring back to a boil, and cook for 8–10 minutes, or following the package directions, until tender but still firm to the bite.

Drain well and add to the meatball sauce, tossing well to coat. Transfer to a warmed serving dish, garnish with the basil leaves and grated Parmesan cheese, and serve immediately.

Bocconcini di pollo pastellati
Chicken nuggets fried in batter

serves 6-8

1 lb 2 oz/500 g skinless, boneless chicken thighs
3 tbsp olive oil
juice of ½ lemon
2 garlic cloves, crushed
8 tbsp all-purpose flour
vegetable oil, for deep-frying
2 eggs, beaten
salt and pepper
coarsely chopped fresh flat-leaf parsley, to garnish
lemon wedges, to serve

Cut the chicken thighs into 1½-inch/4-cm chunks. Mix the olive oil, lemon juice, garlic, and salt and pepper in a bowl. Add the chicken pieces and let marinate at room temperature for an hour, or in the refrigerator overnight

When ready to cook, remove the chicken pieces from the marinade and drain. Spread the flour on a plate and mix with a pinch of salt and plenty of pepper.

Heat the vegetable oil in a deep-fat fryer or large saucepan to 350°F/180°C, or until a cube of bread browns in 30 seconds. Roll the chicken in the seasoned flour and then in the beaten egg. Immediately drop into the hot oil, a few pieces at a time, and deep-fry for about 5 minutes, until golden and crispy, turning occasionally with tongs. Drain on crumpled paper towels. Place the chicken pieces in a warmed serving dish and sprinkle with parsley. Serve hot with thick wedges of lemon.

Tonno con fagioli bianchi e carciofi
Seared tuna with white beans and artichokes

serves 6

2/3 cup extra virgin olive oil
juice of 1 lemon
1/2 tsp dried chile flakes
1/4 tsp pepper
4 thin fresh tuna steaks,
    weighing about 1 lb/450 g
1¼ cups dried cannellini beans,
    soaked overnight
1 shallot, finely chopped
1 garlic clove, crushed
2 tsp finely chopped rosemary
2 tbsp chopped flat-leaf parsley
4 oil-cured artichokes, quartered
4 vine-ripened tomatoes, sliced
    lengthwise into segments
16 black olives, pitted
salt and pepper
lemon wedges, to garnish

Put 4 tablespoons of the olive oil in a shallow dish with 3 tablespoons of the lemon juice and the chile flakes and pepper. Add the tuna steaks and let marinate at room temperature for 1 hour, turning occasionally.

Meanwhile, drain the beans and put in a saucepan with plenty of fresh water to cover. Bring to a boil, then boil rapidly for 15 minutes. Reduce the heat slightly and cook for another 30 minutes, or until tender but not disintegrating. Season with salt in the last 5 minutes of cooking. Drain the beans and place in a bowl. While still warm, toss with 5 tablespoons of the olive oil, then stir in the shallot, garlic, rosemary, parsley, and remaining lemon juice.

Season with salt and pepper. Let stand for at least 30 minutes to let the flavors develop. Heat the remaining oil in a skillet until very hot. Add the tuna and the marinade, and sear for 1–2 minutes each side over very high heat. Remove from the skillet and let cool a little.

Transfer the beans to a serving dish. Mix in the artichokes, tomatoes, and olives, adding more oil and seasoning if necessary. Flake the tuna and arrange on top. Garnish with lemon wedges and serve at room temperature.

Capesante al forno
Baked scallops

serves 6

1 lb 9 oz/700 g shelled scallops, chopped
2 onions, finely chopped
2 garlic cloves, finely chopped
3 tbsp chopped fresh parsley
pinch of freshly grated nutmeg
pinch of ground cloves
2 tbsp fresh white breadcrumbs
2 tbsp olive oil
salt and pepper

Preheat the oven to 400°F/200°C. Mix the scallops, onions, garlic, 2 tablespoons of the parsley, the nutmeg, and the cloves together in a bowl and season with salt and pepper.

Divide the mixture between 4 scrubbed scallop shells or heatproof dishes. Sprinkle the breadcrumbs and remaining parsley on top and drizzle with the olive oil.

Bake the scallops in the preheated oven for 15—20 minutes, or until lightly golden and piping hot. Serve immediately.

Mama's tips for feeding a big family

Remember, Mama's the boss! When you're feeding a big family, you can't bend to their every individual whim. Casa Mama is not a ristorante, there is no menu to choose from!

Families are the root of all Italian life. They make us everything we are. I was one of seven children, and Alberto, my husband, the eldest of five. Now we have six children of our own, and more grandchildren than I have fingers on my hands and toes on both feet together. A big family is a gift — and a big dining table is where we all come together to show our thanks for such a blessing.

My Mama had a saying: " È meglio un uovo oggi che una gallina domani" (an egg today is better than a chicken tomorrow.)

Even if you don't have much, using what you do have with passion and imagination can still be enough for a feast.

Cut your coat according to your cloth. Many hungry mouths can take a lot of feeding — and keeping everyone full and happy means learning to budget.

A big pot will feed more than many individual servings—and good ciabatta will pad out any spaces left by a smaller pot.

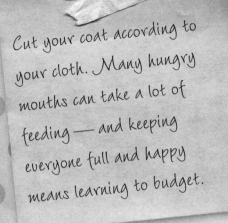

Make mealtimes the focal point of the day. Everyone should sit, eat, drink, talk, and laugh together. From the oldest Mama to the youngest child, meals are there to be shared—and there should be no excuses for missing them.

When you're cooking for many, keep it simple. When we have the children, grandchildren, cousins, nephews, nieces, and even grandcousins for dinner, two or three simple dishes done well — a big salad, maybe, and spaghetti with meatballs — are easier for Mama to handle, and there are fewer dishes for Alberto to wash!

Panna cotta
Vanilla dessert

Cut the vanilla bean lengthwise and scrape out the seeds. In a saucepan, bring the cream to a boil with the vanilla bean and seeds. Stir in the superfine sugar. Simmer over low heat for 15 minutes.

Soak the gelatin in cold water for about 10 minutes, then drain or press the liquid from the gelatin. Pour the hot cream through a strainer into a bowl, then dissolve the gelatin in it.

Rinse 4 small soufflé dishes in cold water and fill with the cream. Chill overnight in the refrigerator. Clean the strawberries, setting aside a few for decoration. Cook the remaining strawberries with the confectioners' sugar. While hot, press the berries through a strainer into a bowl and then let cool. To serve, turn out the soufflé dishes onto dessert plates, dot with strawberry sauce, and decorate with the reserved whole berries.

serves 4

1 vanilla bean
2 cups heavy cream
4½ tbsp superfine sugar
4 sheets clear gelatin
generous 1 lb/500 g
    strawberries
3 tbsp confectioners'
    sugar

Macedonia
Fruit salad

Pit the plums and nectarines and cut into thin wedges. Peel and quarter the pears, remove the cores, and cut into cubes. Place the fruit in a bowl and sprinkle with the lime juice.

Halve the grapes and remove any seeds with the point of a knife. Combine the sugar and vanilla sugar with the orange juice and amaretto. Pour this over the fruit and gently toss so all the fruit is coated. Chill in the refrigerator for 1 hour.

Quarter the figs and place in a bowl with the fruit salad. Serve.

serves 4

5 large black plums
2 nectarines
2 pears
juice of 1 lime
7 oz/200 g red grapes
7 oz/200 g white grapes
2 tbsp superfine sugar
2 tsp vanilla sugar
7 tbsp freshly squeezed
  orange juice
¼ cup amaretto
2 fresh figs

Gelato di albicocche
Apricot ice cream

serves 6

1 lb 2 oz/500 g ripe apricots
1¼ cups light cream
scant 1 cup superfine sugar
scant 1 cup milk
½ tsp vanilla extract

Mama's Tip
If you have an ice cream maker, pour the mixture into the machine and freeze according to the manufacturer's instructions.

Halve the apricots and remove and discard the pits. Put the apricots in a food processor or blender and process until smooth.

Whip together the cream and sugar in a mixing bowl using a handheld electric mixer or a hand whisk until the sugar has dissolved. Whisk in the apricot puree, milk, and vanilla extract. Pour into a freezerproof container that has a lid, then cover and freeze for 1 hour. Remove from the freezer and whisk thoroughly, using a handheld electric mixer or a hand whisk. Re-cover and freeze for an additional hour.

Repeat the whisking and freezing process until the mixture is almost frozen solid. Whisk a final time, then re-cover and return to the freezer until required.

Transfer the ice cream to the refrigerator 15 minutes before serving to soften slightly.

Be my

Valentine

Mama's Celebrations

When it's time for a party in our part of Apulia, the only person allowed to create the party food is Mama. Celebration feasts are as intrinsic to Italian life as vino rosso and opera, and providing the right food, cooked the right way, is all-important.

From Mama's famous risotti and osso buco to unbeatable recipes for chicken, turkey, and duck, the following pages will cover any party, big or small — and Mama's handy tips on "big meal equipment" will prevent any last-minute panics.

Leaving your guests with full bellies and smiles on their faces can be easier than you think — let Mama show you how!

Risotto con gli aspargi
Risotto with asparagus

serves 4

1 lb 2 oz/500 g asparagus
1 pinch of sugar
3 tbsp butter
1 small onion, finely chopped
1½ cups Arborio rice
½ cup white wine
salt and pepper

Remove the woody ends of the asparagus. Cut off the tips and set them aside. Cut the rest of the asparagus into pieces. Bring 4 cups of water to a boil in a saucepan with the sugar, 1 teaspoon of the butter, and a little salt. Blanch the asparagus tips briefly. Remove them with a slotted spoon, refresh in ice water, and set aside. Put the asparagus pieces in the cooking liquid and cook them for 15 minutes. Pour the liquid through a strainer, saving the broth. Puree the asparagus with a handheld electric mixer and keep warm.

Heat 1 tablespoon of butter in a large skillet, add the onion, and sauté. Add the rice, stirring to coat with butter, then deglaze the skillet with the white wine. As soon as the wine has evaporated, pour in one third of the hot asparagus broth, stirring continuously until it is absorbed. Repeat twice. After 15 minutes, add the remaining butter and the asparagus puree, and blend the asparagus tips into the rice. Season with salt and pepper. Remove from the heat, cover, and let rest for 2—3 minutes before serving.

Risotto nero con seppie
Black risotto with squid

serves 4

1 lb 2 oz/500 g squid
1 bunch flat-leaf parsley
4 tbsp olive oil
1 shallot, finely chopped
1 garlic clove, finely chopped
1½ cups Arborio rice
1 cup white wine
4 cups fish stock
salt and pepper

Clean the squid and carefully remove the ink sac from each one. Cut the squid into narrow strips. Cut the stems off the parsley and finely chop the leaves. Bring a small quantity of water to a boil and cook the ink sacs with the parsley stems and a pinch of salt for several minutes. Pass through a strainer and save the liquid.

Heat the olive oil in a saucepan, add the shallots and garlic, and sauté. Add the strips of squid and sauté briefly. Stir in the rice and coat with the oil. Deglaze the pan with the white wine.

Heat the stock in another saucepan. As soon as the wine has evaporated, gradually pour in one third of the hot stock, stirring continuously, until the liquid is absorbed. Repeat this process twice more.

After about 15 minutes, stir in the ink sauce and simmer for a few minutes. Season with salt and pepper and serve sprinkled with the reserved chopped parsley.

Risotto ai funghi porcini
Risotto with porcini

serves 4

10½ oz/300 g porcini mushrooms
2½ oz/75 g prosciutto
3 tbsp butter
2 shallots, finely chopped
1½ cups Arborio rice
1 cup prosecco
4 cups meat stock
salt and pepper
1 tbsp finely chopped parsley, to garnish
2/3 cup grated Parmesan cheese, to serve

Clean and thinly slice the porcini.
Finely dice the prosciutto.

Melt half the butter in a saucepan, add the
shallots and prosciutto, and fry. Sprinkle
the rice into the pan and continue to cook.
Deglaze the pan with the prosecco.

Heat the stock in a separate saucepan.
When the wine has nearly evaporated,
pour in one third of the hot stock,
stirring continuously, until the liquid is
absorbed. Repeat twice more.

Meanwhile, melt the remaining butter in a
saucepan, add the mushrooms, sauté, then
add to the risotto. Season with salt and
pepper. Sprinkle with parsley and serve
with Parmesan cheese.

Mama's tips for the perfect "big Italian" gathering

A celebration without good food is like a summer without sunshine— something that is almost unthinkable in Apulia. Nobody does a celebratory feast like the Italians— and nobody in Italy does it like Mama. And with a little help, you can put on a spread your friends and family will remember for years.

It's not just about the food. Good wine, good conversation, laughter, music, and stories are all essential ingredients.

As much as possible, seat people where everyone can see everyone else. Borrow and improvise: Push tables together to make bigger tables. With good clean, tablecloths and plenty to eat, nobody will notice.

Include the children. Why do some people insist on the little ones eating separately? To Mama that's against nature. With children at the table there is always more joy.

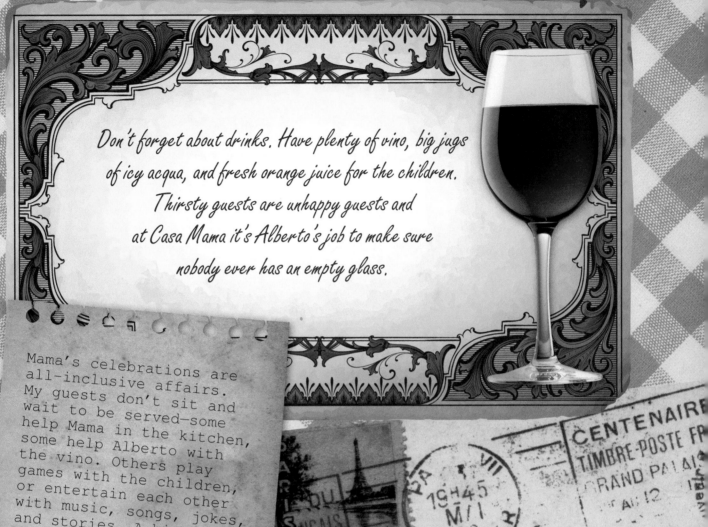

Don't forget about drinks. Have plenty of vino, big jugs of icy acqua, and fresh orange juice for the children. Thirsty guests are unhappy guests and at Casa Mama it's Alberto's job to make sure nobody ever has an empty glass.

Mama's celebrations are all-inclusive affairs. My guests don't sit and wait to be served—some help Mama in the kitchen, some help Alberto with the vino. Others play games with the children, or entertain each other with music, songs, jokes, and stories. A big Italian gathering is not like going to a ristorante. It is a noisy, busy, living thing where everyone is involved.

There is an Italian proverb: "Chi mangia da solo, muore da solo" (he who eats alone, dies alone). Food is best enjoyed in company. Don't save your big gatherings for special occasions — being alive and with people you love is cause enough for celebration.

Don't worry too much about good etiquette. Basic manners are important, of course, but the important thing is that everyone enjoys themselves. Who cares what fork is used, really?

Construite de 1887 à 1889. Hauteur : 300 m Poids : 7 millions de kilos Ecartement à la base : 104 m. 2.500 000 rivets relient ses 15.000 pièces de métal. La 1re plate-forme est à 57 m, la 2e à 115 m. La 3e à 280 m. Les escaliers comportent 1.710 marches.

Melanzane alla campagnola
Country-style marinated eggplant slices

serves 4

4 eggplants
6 tomatoes
2 garlic cloves
1/2 bunch parsley
4 tbsp olive oil,
   plus extra for oiling
salt and pepper

Wash and trim the eggplants, then cut into slices 1/3 inch/1 cm thick. Sprinkle them with salt and place in a strainer to drain for 1 hour.

Preheat the oven to 400°F /200°C. Meanwhile, peel and quarter the tomatoes, remove the seeds, and finely dice the flesh. Peel the garlic and finely chop it, along with the parsley. Add this mixture to the tomatoes, then add salt and pepper. Stir in 2 tablespoons of the olive oil and let marinate.

Lightly oil a baking sheet. Pat the eggplant slices dry with paper towels and arrange them next to each other on the prepared baking sheet. Drizzle over the remaining oil, then roast them in the oven for 5 minutes on each side. Brush the eggplant slices with the tomato mixture and stack them up into little towers to serve.

Polenta e fontina
Cornmeal with fontina

serves 4

4 cups water
1 tsp salt
1¾ cups coarsely ground
   cornmeal
4 tbsp butter,
   plus extra for greasing
6 oz/175 g fontina cheese
freshly ground black pepper
sprigs of rosemary, to garnish

Put the water in a large saucepan with the salt and bring to a boil. Add the cornmeal, stirring continuously, and cook for 5 minutes. Reduce the heat and let the cornmeal simmer for about 30 minutes, stirring continuously, until it no longer sticks to the pan.

Rinse a round baking dish with cold water. Transfer the cornmeal to the dish, spread it smooth, and let cool. Then remove it from the dish and slice through it twice, horizontally to create three even layers. Clean the baking dish and grease it with butter.

Preheat the oven to 400°F/200°C. Thinly slice the cheese. Lay a slice of polenta in the baking dish. Top it with a third of the cheese slices, season with pepper, then cover with the next slice of polenta. Repeat, then spread the rest of the cheese on top. Place little dabs of butter over it. Bake in the preheated oven for 20–25 minutes. Serve with a sprinkling of freshly ground black pepper and garnished with a sprig of rosemary.

Osso buco alla milanese
Milanese-style osso buco

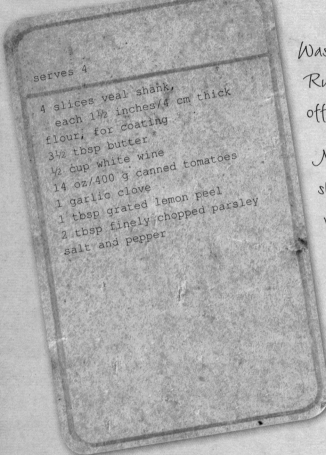

serves 4

4 slices veal shank,
  each 1½ inches/4 cm thick
flour, for coating
3½ tbsp butter
½ cup white wine
14 oz/400 g canned tomatoes
1 garlic clove
1 tbsp grated lemon peel
2 tbsp finely chopped parsley
salt and pepper

Wash the veal slices and pat dry with paper towels. Rub with salt and pepper and coat with flour, shaking off any excess.

Melt the butter in a deep saucepan and brown the veal slices on both sides. Deglaze the pan with the wine, then reduce. Stir in the tomatoes and season with salt and pepper. Cover the pan and stew the meat over low heat for at least 1½ hours, turning the slices over several times in the tomato sauce as they cook.

When the meat begins to separate from the bone, it is done. Finely chop the garlic and combine it with the lemon peel and parsley. Sprinkle over the sliced meat just before serving.

Involtini alla Barese
Beef roulades with pecorino

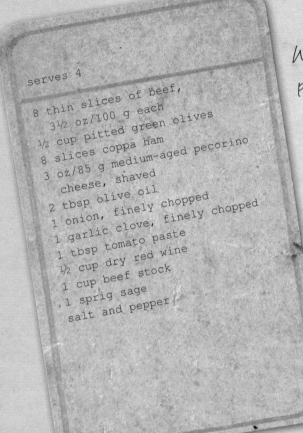

serves 4

8 thin slices of beef,
  3½ oz/100 g each
½ cup pitted green olives
8 slices coppa ham
3 oz/85 g medium-aged pecorino
  cheese, shaved
2 tbsp olive oil
1 onion, finely chopped
1 garlic clove, finely chopped
1 tbsp tomato paste
½ cup dry red wine
1 cup beef stock
1 sprig sage
salt and pepper

Wash the sliced beef, pat it dry with paper towels, and pound flat.

Finely dice the olives. Lightly season the meat with salt and pepper on both sides and cover each slice with a slice of ham. Sprinkle the olives and cheese over the ham.

Roll up the roulades and tie them with kitchen string.

Heat the olive oil in a saucepan and brown the roulades over medium heat. Add the onion, garlic, and tomato paste and sauté.

Deglaze the pan with the wine, stirring to loosen the sediment, and let the liquid reduce.

Pour in the stock, add the sage sprig, cover the pan halfway, and braise for 30—40 minutes over low heat. Take the roulades out of the pan, remove the string, and keep the meat warm. Bring the sauce to a boil and season with salt and pepper. Serve the roulades on warmed plates with the sauce poured over them.

Stracotto di manzo
Beef braised in red wine

serves 6

3 tbsp olive oil
2 onions, finely sliced
2 garlic cloves, chopped
2 lb 4 oz/1 kg braising beef,
    cut into thick strips
2 tbsp all-purpose flour
1½ cups good-quality red wine,
    such as Chianti
2 fresh sage sprigs
1 cup beef stock or
    vegetable stock
1 tbsp tomato paste
salt and pepper
1 tbsp finely chopped fresh
    flat-leaf parsley, to garnish

Preheat the oven to 300°F/150°C. Heat 1 tablespoon of the oil in a large skillet, then add the onions and garlic and cook over medium heat, stirring frequently, for 6—8 minutes, or until softened and browned.

Remove with a slotted spoon and transfer to a casserole. Heat the remaining oil in the skillet, then add the beef strips and cook over high heat, stirring, for 3—4 minutes, or until browned all over. Sprinkle in the flour and stir well to prevent lumps.

Season well with salt and pepper. Reduce the heat to medium, then pour in the wine, stirring continuously, and bring to a boil, continuing to stir.

Carefully turn the contents of the skillet into the casserole. Add the sage, stock, and tomato paste, then cover and cook in the center of the preheated oven for 2½—3 hours. Remove from the oven and discard the sage, then taste and adjust the seasoning if necessary. Sprinkle with parsley and serve.

Mama's Tips
A lamb casserole can be made in the same way. Use lean leg or shoulder of lamb.

Sometimes tougher cuts of meat are braised in Tuscan cooking, often on the stove. But here the beef is cooked in the oven so that it needs little attention.

Spezzatino di maiale
Pork stew

serves 4

1 lb 5 oz/600 g lean pork
2–3 tbsp olive oil
1 tsp fennel seeds
5 garlic cloves, finely chopped
1 fresh red chile, finely chopped
2 medium tomatoes, peeled
    and diced
salt and pepper
sprigs of basil, to garnish

Wash the meat, pat dry with paper towels, and cut into bite-size pieces. Heat the olive oil in a casserole and add the fennel seeds and garlic.

Season the meat with salt and pepper.

Brown the meat on all sides in the hot oil. As soon as the meat browns, add the chile and tomatoes. Cover and stew over low heat for about 1 hour, adding a little warm water as needed. Serve garnished with sprigs of basil.

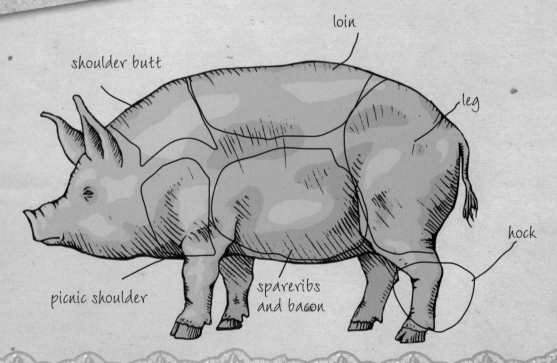

loin

shoulder butt

leg

hock

picnic shoulder

spareribs
and bacon

Pollo alla cacciatora
Chicken cacciatore

serves 4

1 chicken
2 tbsp olive oil
2 oz/55.g pancetta, diced
1 onion, finely chopped
½ cup white wine
4 tomatoes
1 cup meat stock
salt and pepper

Wash the chicken, pat dry with paper towels, and cut into 8 pieces. Rub generous amounts of salt and pepper into the skin. Heat the oil in a casserole, add the pancetta and onion, and fry until the onions are translucent.

Add the chicken pieces and brown on all sides. Deglaze the pot with the white wine and let simmer for 5 minutes.

Peel and quarter the tomatoes, remove the seeds, and cut into small dice. Add to the chicken, then pour in the stock. Cover and cook over low heat for 30—40 minutes. Season with salt and pepper before serving.

Involtini di petti di pollo
Stuffed chicken breasts

serves 4

4 skinless, boneless chicken
  breasts, each weighing about
  5½ oz/150 g
4 thin slices Italian
  dry-cured ham
4 slices pecorino cheese
4 cooked asparagus spears,
  plus extra to serve
1 tbsp all-purpose flour
3 tbsp butter
2 tbsp olive oil
2/3 cup dry white wine
½ cup chicken stock
salt and pepper

Put each chicken breast between two sheets of plastic wrap or inside a plastic food bag and, using a rolling pin, gently beat out until 3/8 inch/8 mm thick. Season well with salt and pepper and place a slice of ham on top of each breast.

Top each with a slice of cheese and an asparagus spear. Roll up carefully and secure with kitchen string. Dust with flour and season well with salt and pepper.

Heat 2 tablespoons of the butter with the oil in a large skillet. Add the chicken rolls and cook over medium heat, turning frequently, for 15 minutes, or until cooked through, tender, and golden brown.

Remove the string, then transfer the chicken rolls to a warmed serving dish and keep warm. Add the wine and stock to the skillet and bring to a boil, scraping up and stirring in any sediment from the bottom of the skillet. Bring to a boil and add the remaining butter. Stir well and let bubble until thick.

Spoon the sauce over the chicken and serve immediately, with extra asparagus spears.

Mama's Tip
You can use Marsala
instead of white wine
to give a different flavor.

Anatra con verdure
Duck with vegetables

serves 4-6

1 young duck, about 3 lb/1.3 kg
1 onion
1 bay leaf
3 cloves
1 bouquet garni
5 peppercorns
5 allspice berries
   (Jamaica peppercorns)
3 medium carrots
1 lb/450 g thick parsley root
2 tbsp olive oil
1 cup veal stock
2 tbsp finely chopped parsley
salt and pepper, plus extra
   sprigs to garnish

Wash the duck and place it in a large saucepan. Spike the onion with the bay leaf and cloves, then add it and the bouquet garni to the pan. Add enough water to cover the duck completely. Season with salt and pepper and add the allspice berries.

Bring to a boil, skimming off the foam that forms on the surface, and simmer over low heat for about 1¼ hours. Cut the carrots and parsley roots into pieces of equal size. Heat the olive oil in a saucepan, add the vegetables, and sauté, then pour over the stock, cover the pan, and cook for 10 minutes. Season with salt and pepper and mix in the parsley. Keep the vegetables warm.

Remove the duck from the broth and let drain well. Remove the skin. Bone the breast meat and legs, then slice. Serve the duck meat and vegetables on a warmed serving platter, garnished with a sprig of parsley.

Vongole veraci marinate
Marinated clams

serves 4

2 lb 4 oz/1 kg fresh clams
1 onion
2 garlic cloves
1/3 cup olive oil
1 cup dry white wine
1 tbsp finely chopped parsley
juice of 1/2 lemon
salt and pepper

Scrub the clam shells. Soak them in cold water for 1 hour, changing the water several times. Discard any clams that have open shells. Peel the onion and garlic and finely dice.

Heat 2 tablespoons of the oil in a large saucepan, add the onions and garlic, and sauté until translucent. Deglaze the pan with the wine and bring to a boil. Add the clams, cover, and cook over high heat for 3–4 minutes, shaking the pot several times.

Remove the clams from the pan with a slotted spoon, discarding any that have not opened, and place in a bowl. Stir in the parsley, lemon juice, and remaining olive oil, and season with salt and pepper. Marinate for 30 minutes, then serve.

Carciofi e frutti di mare
Artichokes with seafood

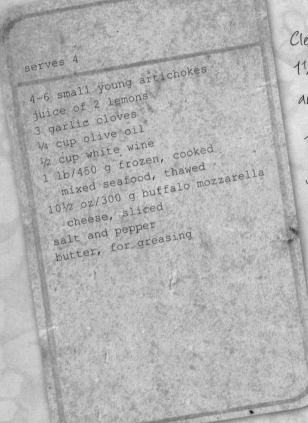

serves 4

4-6 small young artichokes
juice of 2 lemons
3 garlic cloves
1/4 cup olive oil
1/2 cup white wine
1 lb/450 g frozen, cooked
    mixed seafood, thawed
10½ oz/300 g buffalo mozzarella
    cheese, sliced
salt and pepper
butter, for greasing

Clean the artichokes, cut the stems to a length of 1½ inches/4 cm, and peel. Remove the tough, outer leaves and slice off the thistles from the inner leaves.

Fill a bowl with 4 cups of water and add the lemon juice. Cut the artichokes lengthwise into thin slices and immediately drop them into the lemon water.

Let them soak for 10 minutes, then pour off the water and drain well. Cut the garlic into slices. Heat the olive oil in a nonstick saucepan and fry the garlic until golden brown, then remove and discard it.

Sauté the artichoke slices in the olive oil, stirring continuously. Season with salt and pepper, then add the white wine. Cover the pan and gently braise the artichokes over medium heat for about 30 minutes, shaking the pan several times as they cook. Meanwhile, preheat the oven to 425°F/220°C and grease a baking dish with butter.

Place the artichoke slices in the baking dish and pour over the cooking juices. Add the seafood and top with cheese slices. Bake in the preheated oven for 20—25 minutes, until the cheese starts to brown. Serve immediately.

Gamberi in padella
Pan-fried shrimp

serves 4

4 garlic cloves
20-24 large, raw shrimp, peeled
scant ½ cup butter
4 tbsp olive oil
6 tbsp brandy
salt and pepper
2 tbsp chopped fresh parsley,
    to garnish
lemon wedges, to serve

Using a sharp knife, peel and slice the garlic.

Wash the shrimp and pat dry with paper towels.

Melt the butter with the oil in a large skillet, add the garlic and shrimp, and fry over high heat, stirring, for 3—4 minutes, until the shrimp are pink.

Add the brandy and season with salt and pepper. Sprinkle with chopped parsley and serve immediately with lemon wedges.

Mama's essential big meal equipment

Big meals mean big planning. Before you start to cook, get your kitchen organized, decluttered, and free from interference from the likes of Alberto. Make a list of everything you need and lay it all out ready — down to the last spoon.

You can never have too many wooden spoons. I keep mine in two big old olive oil cans—one group for sweet things, the other for savory.

Love your knives. In the kitchen, you're nothing without your knives. They're not just for chopping, they're the tools with which you express your creativity and passion for food. Nurture them, keep them clean and sharp. Look after them like a sculptor looks after his chisels, like an artist looks after his brushes. Without them you're no cook at all.

Keep different cutting boards for different flavors. Mama keeps four: One for fish, one for meat, one for vegetables, and a thick wooden one for bread and cheese.

Get the biggest baking dishes and roasting pans your oven can handle—and the best you can afford. If you're cooking for friends, family, and half the village like Mama seems to, they're worth their weight in gold.

Every cook should have at least one big stockpot. The best kind are those that can be used on the stove and in the oven—not only are they perfect for making the kinds of big wholesome stews that work so well for large numbers, but they mean that even with a small oven you can keep two in use at the same time.

Remember, the best cooking equipment can't be found in the stores. Your senses are the truest guide of all: use your eyes, nose, and, most important, your taste buds.

Tiramisù bianco con fragole
White tiramisu with strawberries

serves 6

2 eggs, separated
3/4 cup confectioners' sugar,
    sifted
1½ cups mascarpone cheese
6 tbsp milk
½ cup Marsala
20 ladyfingers
1/3 cup chopped almonds
2 oz/55 g white chocolate,
    coarsely grated
fresh strawberries, halved,
    to serve

Whisk the egg yolks with the sugar in a mixing bowl with a handheld electric mixer or hand whisk until thick and creamy. Add the mascarpone cheese and whisk into the egg yolk mixture.

Whisk the egg whites in a separate mixing bowl and then fold into the mascarpone mixture.

Pour the milk into a shallow dish and add the Marsala. Dip the ladyfingers into the milk mixture just long enough to soften, then arrange half the dipped ladyfingers in the bottom of a baking dish 9–10 inches/23–25 cm in diameter. Sprinkle over half the almonds. Spread over a third of the mascarpone mixture and top with a layer of the remaining dipped ladyfingers and the remaining nuts. Spoon the remaining mascarpone mixture over the top and swirl to give an attractive appearance. Cover with plastic wrap and chill in the refrigerator for 2–3 hours.

To serve, remove from the refrigerator and decorate with the white chocolate and strawberries.

Pere con Marsala
Poached pears in Marsala

serves 4

4 firm pears,
   such as Comice
1/4 cup superfine sugar
2 cinnamon sticks
1/2 cup Marsala
1/2 cup sour cream, to serve

Carefully peel the pears. Cut a slice from the bottom of each pear and discard, then remove and discard the core from each pear, using a pointed knife. Put the prepared pears in a saucepan, add enough water to just cover, then add the sugar and cinnamon sticks.

Slowly bring to a boil over low heat, stirring until the sugar has dissolved.

Cover and simmer gently until the pears are tender. This will take from 20—40 minutes, depending on their firmness. Remove from the heat. Using a slotted spoon, transfer the pears to a serving dish. Remove the cinnamon sticks. Return the pan to the heat and let the liquid simmer for 2—3 minutes, or until thickened. Stir in the Marsala and pour over the pears.

Serve warm, or cover and let chill in the refrigerator before serving with sour cream.

Mama's Tip
Pears can also be poached in red wine or white wine.

Pears are a popular fruit in Tuscan cooking and are frequently served as part of a salad, often with walnuts and cheese. Here they are poached in Marsala until tender.

Panforte di Siena
Tuscan Christmas cake

serves 12–14

generous ¾ cup hazelnuts
generous ¾ cup almonds
½ cup candied peel
⅓ cup dried apricots,
    finely chopped
⅓ cup candied pineapple,
    finely chopped
grated rind of 1 orange
scant ½ cup all-purpose flour
2 tbsp unsweetened cocoa
1 tsp ground cinnamon
¼ tsp ground coriander
¼ tsp freshly grated nutmeg
¼ tsp ground cloves
generous ½ cup superfine sugar
½ cup honey
confectioners' sugar, to decorate

Preheat the oven to 350°F/180°C. Line an 8-inch/20-cm round springform cake pan with parchment paper. Spread out the hazelnuts on a baking sheet and toast in the preheated oven for 10 minutes, until golden brown. Turn them onto a dish towel and rub off the skins. Meanwhile, spread out the almonds on a baking sheet and toast in the oven for 10 minutes, until golden, watching carefully, because they can burn easily.

Reduce the oven temperature to 300°F/150°C. Chop all the nuts and place in a large bowl. Add the candied peel, apricots, pineapple, and orange rind to the nuts and mix well. Sift the flour, cocoa, cinnamon, coriander, nutmeg, and cloves together into the bowl and mix well.

Put the sugar and honey into a saucepan and set over low heat, stirring, until the sugar has dissolved. Bring to a boil and cook for 5 minutes, until thickened and starting to darken. Stir the nut mixture into the pan and remove from the heat.

Spoon the mixture into the prepared cake pan and level the surface with the back of a damp spoon. Bake in the oven for 1 hour, then transfer to a wire rack to cool in the pan.

Carefully remove the cake from the pan and peel off the lining paper. Just before serving, dredge the top with confectioners' sugar. Cut into thin wedges to serve.

Mama's Comfort Food

Cooking is not all about taking care of others — Mama loves to look after Alberto and the children, but she also has to look after herself! Comfort food is for those days when you're a little down, when you need cheering up, and also for the times when all you really want to do is relax with something easy to make and delicious to eat. Pizza, ravioli, frittata, a wholesome seafood stew — and a panettone bread and butter pudding to warm every bone in your body.

This chapter is "Mama's cibo per l'anima": (food for the soul).

My favorite pizzas

Basic pizza dough

makes 4 individual pizzas
2 envelopes active dry
  yeast
½ tsp sugar
½ cup lukewarm water,
  plus 5-7 tbsp water
3 cups all-purpose flour,
  plus extra for dusting
1 tsp salt
3 tbsp olive oil

Crumble the yeast into a
small bowl and sprinkle
with the sugar. Add the
½ cup of lukewarm water,
then stir to dissolve the
yeast and sugar. Cover with
a clean dish towel and let
rise in a warm spot for
30 minutes. Sift the flour
into a large bowl. Make a
hollow in the center and
pour the yeast mixture,
salt, olive oil, and the
remaining water into it.
Knead everything into a
smooth, silky dough, then
shape it into a ball. Dust
the ball with a little
flour, cover, and set aside
in a warm place to rise
for an additional hour, or
until doubled in volume.

Pizza alla marinara
Mariner's pizza

serves 4
1 quantity basic pizza dough
flour, for dusting
1 lb 10 oz/800 g canned
  chopped tomatoes
3-4 garlic cloves, finely chopped
1 tbsp oregano
2 oz/55 g capers
½ cup pitted black olives
7 oz/200 g Bel Paese cheese, grated
3 tbsp olive oil, plus extra
  for greasing
salt and pepper

Preheat the oven to 425°F/220°C and
grease 4 small, round pizza pans.
Divide the dough into four equal
portions and roll them into circles on
a floured counter. Place the circles
of dough on the prepared pans.

Distribute the tomatoes over the
dough. Season with the garlic,
oregano, and salt and pepper. Scatter
over the capers and olives and
sprinkle with the grated cheese.
Drizzle over the oil, then bake in the
preheated oven for about 20 minutes.

Pizza quattro stagioni
Four seasons pizza

serves 4
1 tbsp butter
3²⁄₃ cups sliced mushrooms
4 tomatoes
7 oz/200 g cooked ham
7 oz/200 g mozzarella cheese
4 artichoke hearts in oil
16 pitted black olives
1 tsp oregano
1 quantity basic pizza dough
flour, for dusting
4 tbsp olive oil, plus extra for greasing
salt and pepper

Preheat the oven to 425°F/220°C and grease
4 small, round pizza pans. Heat the butter in
a skillet, add the mushrooms, and sauté for
10 minutes. Peel, quarter, and seed the
tomatoes, then cut them into small dice. Cut
the ham into small pieces. Thinly slice the
cheese. Quarter the artichoke hearts.

Divide the dough into four equal portions
and roll them out into circles on a floured
counter. Place the circles in the pans.

Distribute the tomatoes and cheese evenly
among the pizzas. Cover one quarter of each
pizza with one of the following toppings:
mushrooms, ham, artichokes, olives. Season
with the oregano and salt and pepper and
drizzle over the oil. Bake in the preheated
oven for about 20 minutes.

Pizza Margherita

serves 4
1 quantity basic pizza dough
⅓ cup olive oil, plus extra
   for greasing
2 small onions, diced
14 oz/400 g canned diced tomatoes
scant 2 cups strained tomatoes
1 tsp oregano
14 oz/400 g mozzarella cheese
salt and pepper
flour, for dusting
basil leaves, to garnish

Heat 4 tablespoons of the oil in a heavy-bottom
saucepan, add the onions, and sauté until
translucent. Add the canned tomatoes, strained
tomatoes, and oregano, and season with salt
and pepper. Cook the sauce for about 30 minutes
over medium heat.

Preheat the oven to 425°F/220°C and grease
4 small, round pizza pans. Divide the dough
into four equal portions and roll them out into
circles on a floured counter. Place the circles
in the pans.

Thinly slice the cheese. Brush the dough with
the tomato sauce, lay the cheese slices on top,
and drizzle over the remaining olive oil. Bake
in the preheated oven for about 20 minutes,
then garnish with basil leaves and serve
immediately.

Frittata con prezzemolo
Frittata with parsley

Beat the eggs in a bowl with some salt and pepper until foaming, then blend in the parsley.

Heat the olive oil in a heavy-bottom skillet until it starts to smoke. Pour in the eggs and smooth the surface with a wooden spatula. Reduce the heat to low and let the eggs thicken.

As soon as the frittata begins to brown on the underside, use a plate to carefully turn over the frittata. Cook the other side until it is golden brown.

Cut the frittata into 4 slices and serve while hot or warm.

serves 4

6 eggs
1 bunch flat-leaf parsley, coarsely chopped
4 tbsp olive oil
salt and pepper

Omelette agli spinaci e mozzarella
Spinach and mozzarella omelet

serves 4

1 tbsp butter
4 eggs, lightly beaten
1½ oz./40 g mozzarella cheese,
   thinly sliced and cut into
   bite-size pieces
small handful baby spinach,
   stalks removed
salt and pepper
1 oil-cured red bell pepper,
   sliced into strips,
   to garnish

Heat a 10-inch/25-cm nonstick skillet over medium—high heat. Add the butter and, when it sizzles, pour in the eggs. Season with salt and pepper, then stir gently with the back of a fork until large flakes form. Let cook for a few seconds, then tilt the skillet and lift the edges of the mixture with a spatula, so that the uncooked egg flows underneath.

Scatter the cheese and spinach over the top and let cook for a few seconds. Once the surface starts to solidify, carefully fold the omelet in half. Cook for a few seconds, pressing the surface with a spatula.

Turn over and cook for another few seconds, until the cheese is soft and the spinach wilted. Transfer the omelet onto a warmed serving dish and slice into segments. Garnish with strips of bell pepper before serving.

Mama's top 10 tips for staying cheerful

1 Mama's philosophy is molto simple. Happy is as happy does. Cooking makes you happy? So cook. Reading makes you happy? Read. Football, opera, art make you happy? So play, sing, paint. Life is there to be enjoyed.

2 Spend some time outdoors every day. Feeling fresh air, sunshine, even rain on our faces reminds us we're alive—and that to be alive is the most wonderful thing of all.

3 Talk to children. The laughter of children is more intoxicating than wine.

4 Count your blessings. It's a cliché? The world was built on clichés! No matter how bad things seem, there are upsides—Mama's rule is that if you can think of enough to run out of fingers to count them on, you've enough good fortune to last the rest of your life.

5 Keep active. Stand still too long and you might begin to think it's not worth moving again.

6 Stay optimistic. Keep doing the right things well and things usually turn out okay.

7 Keep your family close, and if you can't stay close physically then talk or write often. Two of my boys work far away in the city of Bari but Gianluca, the youngest, says that with his cell phone and something called e-mail he can stay in touch every day. I have no idea what any of it really means but it sounds wonderful.

8 Close your eyes and eat a grape, an olive, some mozzarella cheese, a sun-dried tomato. Instant happiness!

9 Remember: Life is not supposed to be easy, but it's not supposed to be miserable either. Misfortunes happen, sadness and grief follow us—but then so does incredible joy. So do laughter, love, beauty, warmth, comfort—even the simple pleasures of a good ciabatta and a toast of vino rosso with a man like Alberto can be enough to make up for whatever else the world throws at us.

10 A full stomach makes a contented mind. Alberto is the happiest man I know—and he eats the best in all Italy.

serves 4

1 lb/450 g fresh spinach
1 cup ricotta cheese
1 egg, beaten
2 tsp fennel seeds,
    lightly crushed
1¾ oz/50 g pecorino cheese or
    Parmesan cheese, finely
    grated, plus extra to garnish
3 tbsp all-purpose flour,
    mixed with 1 tsp dried thyme
5 tbsp butter
2 garlic cloves, crushed
salt and pepper
tomato wedges, to serve

Wash the spinach and trim off any long stalks. Place in a large saucepan, cover, and cook for 4—5 minutes, until wilted. This will probably have to be done in batches because the volume of spinach is large. Place in a colander to drain and cool.

Mash the ricotta cheese and beat in the egg and the fennel seeds. Season with plenty of salt and pepper, then stir in the pecorino cheese.

Squeeze as much excess water as possible from the spinach and finely chop the leaves. Stir the spinach into the cheese mixture. Take about 1 tablespoon of the spinach-and-cheese mixture, shape it into a ball, and flatten it slightly to form a patty. Gently roll in the seasoned flour. Continue until all of the mixture has been used up.

Fill a large skillet halfway with water and bring to a boil. Carefully add the patties and cook for 3—4 minutes, or until they rise to the surface. Remove with a slotted spoon.

Melt the butter in a small saucepan. Add the garlic and cook for 2—3 minutes. Pour the garlic butter over the patties, season with pepper, and serve at once with the tomato wedges, and grated cheese.

Mozzarella in carrozza
Deep-fried mozzarella

serves 4

8 slices bread, preferably
   slightly stale, crusts removed
4 oz/100 g mozzarella cheese,
   thickly sliced
⅓ cup chopped, pitted black
   olives
8 canned anchovy fillets,
   drained and chopped
16 fresh basil leaves, plus extra
   to garnish
4 eggs, beaten
⅔ cup milk
salt and pepper
oil, for deep-frying

Cut each slice of bread into 2 triangles. Top 8 of the bread triangles with equal amounts of the cheese, olives, and chopped anchovies. Place the basil leaves on top and season with salt and pepper.

Lay the remaining 8 triangles of bread over the top and press down around the edges to seal.

Mix the eggs and milk together and pour into an ovenproof dish. Add the sandwiches and let soak for about 5 minutes.

Add oil to a large saucepan and heat to 350–375°F/180–190°C, or until a cube of bread browns in 30 seconds.

Before cooking the sandwiches, squeeze the edges together again. Carefully place them in the oil and deep-fry for 2 minutes, or until golden, turning once. Remove the sandwiches with a slotted spoon and drain on paper towels. You will have to cook the sandwiches in batches. Serve immediately while still hot, garnished with a few basil leaves.

Patate e finocchio al forno
Potato and fennel bake

serves 6

2 lb 4 oz/1 kg potatoes
2-3 fennel bulbs
4 tbsp olive oil
1 onion, finely chopped
2 garlic cloves, crushed
4 fresh sage leaves
2/3 cup dry white wine
salt and pepper

Preheat the oven to 400°F/200°C. Peel then finely slice the potatoes. Trim then finely slice the fennel.

Oil a large gratin dish with half the oil. Layer half the potato slices in the bottom of the prepared dish and season well with salt and pepper. Sprinkle over half the onion and garlic and cover with the fennel. Sprinkle the remaining onion and garlic over and season again with salt and pepper. Tuck the sage leaves into the vegetables. Finish with a neat layer of the potato slices and season again with salt and pepper.

Pour over the wine and drizzle over the remaining oil. Cover the dish with foil and bake in the preheated oven for 30 minutes. Remove the foil and bake for an additional 20—30 minutes, or until the potatoes are brown and crisp.

Mama's Tip

You can use a food processor fitted with a slicer attachment for slicing the potatoes, but a mandolin is the ideal tool to use.

Ravioli alla zucca
Pumpkin ravioli

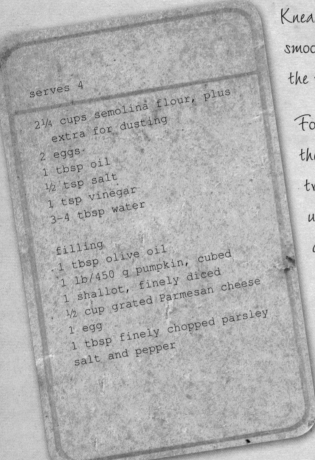

serves 4

2¼ cups semolina flour, plus
    extra for dusting
2 eggs
1 tbsp oil
½ tsp salt
1 tsp vinegar
3-4 tbsp water

filling
1 tbsp olive oil
1 lb/450 g pumpkin, cubed
1 shallot, finely diced
½ cup grated Parmesan cheese
1 egg
1 tbsp finely chopped parsley
salt and pepper

Knead the flour, eggs, oil, salt, vinegar, and water into a silky smooth dough. Wrap the dough in plastic wrap and chill in the refrigerator for 1 hour.

For the filling, heat the olive oil in a saucepan, add the pumpkin and shallot, and sauté until the shallot is translucent. Add ½ cup of water and cook the pumpkin until the liquid evaporates. Cool slightly, then mix with the cheese, egg, parsley, and salt and pepper.

Divide the dough in half. Thinly roll out both pieces. Place small spoonfuls of the pumpkin mixture about 1½ inches/4 cm apart on one sheet of dough. Brush a little water on the spaces in between. Lay the second sheet of dough on top and press down around each piece of filling. Use a pastry wheel to cut out squares and press the edges together with a fork.

Let the ravioli dry for 30 minutes, then bring a large saucepan of lightly salted water to a boil. Add the ravioli and cook over medium heat until tender, but firm to the bite. Remove them with a slotted spoon and drain well on paper towels.

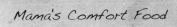

Ravioli al formaggio
Ravioli with feta cheese

serves 4
2¼ cups semolina flour, plus extra for dusting
2 eggs
1 tbsp oil
½ tsp salt
1 tsp vinegar
3-4 tbsp water

filling
9 oz/250 g feta cheese
2 garlic cloves, finely chopped
2 tbsp finely chopped parsley
1 fresh red chile,
    seeded and finely chopped
salt and pepper

Knead the flour, eggs, oil, salt, vinegar, and water
into a silky smooth dough. Wrap the dough in plastic
wrap and chill in the refrigerator for 1 hour.
For the filling, crumble the cheese and combine it
with the garlic, parsley, and chile. Season with salt
and pepper. Prepare the ravioli in the same way as for
Ravioli alla zucca (page 108).

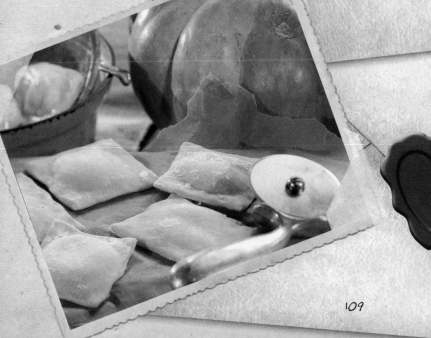

Farfalle con pomodori secchi e basilico
Farfalle with sun-dried tomatoes

serves 4

1 oz/30 g sun-dried tomatoes
1/4 cup pine nuts
1 handful fresh basil
2 garlic cloves, chopped
generous 1/3 cup olive oil
1 tbsp grated Parmesan cheese
14 oz/400 g dried farfalle pasta
salt and pepper

Pour hot water over the sun-dried tomatoes and soak them for 25 minutes. Then pour off the water, squeeze out the liquid, and chop.

Roast the pine nuts in dry skillet until golden brown. Grind half of the pine nuts with the basil leaves, garlic, and 1/2 teaspoon of salt in a large mortar. Gradually work in the olive oil, then add the cheese.

Stir the chopped tomatoes into the basil sauce.

Bring a large saucepan of lightly salted water to a boil. Add the pasta and cook according to the package directions until tender, but still firm to the bite. Drain the pasta and combine it, still dripping wet, with the basil-tomato sauce in a warmed bowl. Serve on warmed plates, seasoned with pepper and sprinkled with the remaining pine nuts.

Cannelloni agli spinaci
Spinach cannelloni

serves 4

12 cannelloni or other large
   pasta tubes
1 lb 5 oz/600 g spinach
1½ tbsp butter, plus extra
   for greasing
1 small onion, finely chopped
generous ¾ cup ricotta
   cheese
freshly grated nutmeg
2½ cups store-bought
   béchamel sauce
½ cup grated Parmesan cheese
salt and pepper

Preheat the oven to 400°F/200°C and grease a baking dish. Bring a large saucepan of lightly salted water to a boil. Add the pasta and cook according to the package directions until firm, but tender to the bite. Drain, rinse under cold running water, then drain again. Wash the spinach thoroughly and remove any wilted leaves and coarse stems.

Meanwhile, heat the butter in a saucepan, add the onion, and sauté until translucent. Add the spinach while still dripping wet, cover the pan, and let the leaves wilt. Drain the spinach well in a strainer, then chop it. Combine the spinach and ricotta cheese, then season with salt, pepper, and nutmeg. Transfer the spinach mixture to a pastry bag with a large nozzle and use it to fill the cannelloni tubes.

Lay the filled cannelloni side by side in the baking dish, cover with the béchamel sauce, and sprinkle with cheese. Bake in the preheated oven for 25—30 minutes.

Gnocchi alla Romana
Roman-style gnocchi

serves 4

2 cups milk
1²/₃ cups water
scant 1 cup butter, plus extra
  for greasing
1³/₄ cups semolina flour
scant 1 cup grated Parmesan
  cheese
2 egg yolks
freshly grated nutmeg
2 tbsp grated fontina cheese
salt and pepper

Combine the milk, water, 2 tablespoons of butter, and ½ teaspoon of salt in a large saucepan and bring to a boil. Gradually sprinkle in the semolina and cook over low heat for 25—30 minutes, stirring continuously. Transfer the mixture to a bowl and stir in 2 tablespoons of the Parmesan cheese and the egg yolks. Season with salt, pepper, and nutmeg. Set aside to cool.

Preheat the oven to 400°F/200°C and grease a baking dish. Use two spoons to form gnocchi from the semolina dough and set them in the baking dish. Mix the remaining Parmesan cheese with the fontina cheese and sprinkle over the gnocchi. Melt the remaining butter and pour it over the cheese.

Bake the gnocchi in the preheated oven for about 20 minutes, until golden brown.

Quadrucci

Fettucine

Ragù alla Bolognese
Bolognese sauce

serves 4

1 oz/25 g dried porcini mushrooms
½ cup lukewarm water
1 tbsp butter
2 oz/50 g pancetta, diced
1 small onion, finely chopped
1 garlic clove, finely chopped
2 small carrots, finely diced
2 celery stalks, finely diced
10½ oz/300 g ground beef
1 pinch of sugar
freshly grated nutmeg
1 tbsp tomato paste
½ cup red wine
generous 1 cup strained tomatoes
salt and pepper

Soak the porcini in the lukewarm water for 20 minutes. Melt the butter in a saucepan, add the pancetta, and fry.

Add the onion and garlic and fry until the onion is translucent. Stir in the carrots and celery and cook for a few minutes, stirring frequently.

Add the beef and fry, stirring continuously. Season with salt and pepper, a pinch of sugar, and some nutmeg. Stir in the tomato paste and cook for a minute or two, then add the red wine. Mix in the strained tomatoes. Thinly slice the porcini and add them to the sauce. Pour the soaking water through a fine strainer into the sauce. Thicken the sauce by cooking it over low heat for 1 hour.

Tagliatelle

Lasagna

Spaghetti

Farfalle

Penne

Fusilli

Conchiglie

Cannelloni

Capelli d'Angelo

117

Spaghetti alla carbonara
Spaghetti carbonara

serves 4

14 oz/400 g dried spaghetti
4 eggs
4 tbsp heavy cream
1/2 cup grated Parmesan cheese
1/2 cup grated pecorino cheese
1 tbsp butter
5 oz/150 g pancetta, finely diced
salt and pepper

Bring a large saucepan of lightly salted water to a boil. Add the pasta and cook according to the package instructions until tender, but firm to the bite.

Meanwhile, stir together the eggs, cream, Parmesan cheese, and pecorino cheese in a bowl. Season with salt and pepper.

Melt the butter in a large saucepan, add the pancetta, and fry until crispy. Drain the spaghetti and add it to the pan while still dripping wet. Pour the cheese sauce over it. Remove the pan from the heat. Toss the pasta in the sauce until the eggs begin to thicken but are still creamy. Serve on warmed plates, sprinkled with pepper.

Lasagne al forno
Beef lasagna with ricotta and mozzarella

serves 6

3/4 cup olive oil
4 tbsp butter
1/2 cup diced bacon or pancetta
1 onion, finely chopped
1 celery stalk, finely chopped
1 carrot, finely chopped
12 oz/350 g beef pot roast,
   in a single piece
5 tbsp red wine
2 tbsp sun-dried tomato paste
7 oz/200 g Italian sausage
2 eggs
1 1/3 cups freshly grated Parmesan
   cheese
1/2 cup fresh breadcrumbs
1 1/2 cups ricotta cheese
8 dried lasagna sheets
12 oz/350 g mozzarella cheese,
   sliced
salt and pepper
chopped fresh parsley, to garnish

Heat 1/2 cup of the oil with the butter in a large saucepan. Add the bacon, onion, celery, and carrot and cook over low heat, until softened. Increase the heat to medium, add the beef, and cook until evenly browned. Stir in the wine and tomato paste, season with salt and pepper, and bring to a boil. Reduce the heat, cover, and simmer gently for 1 1/2 hours, until the beef is tender.

Meanwhile, heat 2 tablespoons of the remaining oil in a skillet. Add the sausage and cook for 8—10 minutes. Remove from the skillet and discard the skin. Thinly slice the sausage and set aside. Transfer the beef to a cutting board and finely dice. Return half the beef to the sauce.

Mix the remaining beef in a bowl with 1 egg, 1 tablespoon of the Parmesan cheese, and the breadcrumbs. Shape into walnut-size balls. Heat the remaining oil in a skillet, add the meatballs, and cook for 5—8 minutes, until browned. Pass the ricotta through a strainer into a bowl. Stir in the remaining egg and 4 tablespoons of the Parmesan cheese.

Preheat the oven to 350°F/180°C. Meanwhile, bring a large saucepan of lightly salted water to a boil. Add the pasta and cook according to the package directions until firm, but tender to the bite. Drain, rinse under cold running water, then drain again. In a rectangular ovenproof dish, make layers with the lasagna sheets, ricotta mixture, meat sauce, meatballs, sausage, and mozzarella cheese. Finish with a layer of the ricotta mixture and sprinkle with the remaining Parmesan cheese.

Bake the lasagna in the preheated oven for 20—25 minutes, until cooked through and bubbling. Serve immediately, garnished with chopped parsley.

Fritto misto di mare
Lightly battered and fried fish

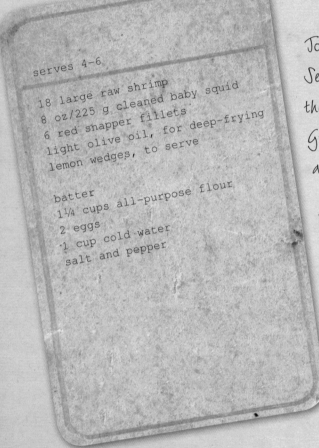

serves 4-6

18 large raw shrimp
8 oz/225 g cleaned baby squid
6 red snapper fillets
light olive oil, for deep-frying
lemon wedges, to serve

batter
1¼ cups all-purpose flour
2 eggs
1 cup cold water
salt and pepper

To make the batter, sift the flour into a mixing bowl. Season the flour with salt and pepper and make a well in the center. Break the eggs into the well and add the water. Gradually beat the eggs and water into the flour to form a smooth batter.

Shell and devein the shrimp. Cut the squid into tentacles and rings and cut the red snapper into small squares.

Heat the oil in a deep-fat fryer or a large heavy-bottomed saucepan to 350—375°F/180—190°C, or until a cube of bread browns in 30 seconds. Dip the seafood in the batter and wipe off any excess. Add to the hot oil, in small batches, and cook for 2—3 minutes, or until crisp and golden. Remove with a slotted spoon, then drain on paper towels and keep warm while you cook the remaining seafood.

Pile onto warmed plates and season with salt, then serve with lemon wedges.

Il cacciucco alla Livornese

Livorno seafood stew

Cut the red snapper fillets into thirds. Cut the monkfish into similar-size pieces, cutting the flesh away from the tailbone (this can be used to make stock). Cut the squid into thick rings and retain the tentacles. Heat the oil in a large saucepan, then add the onion, garlic, and fennel and cook over medium heat, stirring frequently, for 4—5 minutes, or until starting to soften. Pour in the wine and stir well, then let simmer until almost evaporated. Add the tomatoes and bring to a boil, then reduce the heat and simmer, uncovered, for 10—15 minutes, or until the fennel is tender and the sauce is reduced and thickened.

serves 6

4 red snapper fillets
1 lb/450 g monkfish tail
14 oz/400 g cleaned baby squid
3 tbsp olive oil
1 onion, finely chopped
2 garlic cloves, finely chopped
2 fennel bulbs, finely sliced
2/3 cup dry white wine
1 lb 5 oz/600 g canned chopped tomatoes
scant 3 cups fish stock
1 lb 2 oz/500 g mussels, scrubbed and debearded
18 large raw shrimp, shelled and deveined
salt and pepper

To serve
2 tbsp finely chopped fresh flat-leaf parsley
6 slices ciabatta bread, toasted, rubbed with garlic, and drizzled with olive oil

Meanwhile, bring the stock to a boil in a separate large saucepan, then add the mussels and cook, covered, over high heat for 3—4 minutes, shaking the pan occasionally, until the mussels have opened. Discard any that remain closed. Strain the mussels, reserving the stock. Remove half the mussels from their shells, discarding the shells. Keep all the mussels warm. Add the reserved stock to the tomato mixture and bring to a boil. Add the snapper, monkfish, squid, and shrimp to the pan and cook for 2—3 minutes, or until tender and the shrimp have turned pink. Add the shelled and unshelled mussels and heat through. Season with salt and pepper.

Divide evenly among individual warmed soup dishes and sprinkle with parsley. Serve each dish with the toasted bread slices.

Mama's tips for taking it easy

Good cooking can't be rushed: bread needs time to rise, flavors need space to infuse properly. Standing over the stove worrying will not make things happen any quicker. Learn to love the wait: it's where the magic happens!

In Italy we say that "La calma è la virtù dei forti" (calm is the virtue of the strong.) Nowhere is this more true than in Mama's kitchen.

Slow down. Why is the younger generation always in such a hurry? My children's children, my children, are forever rushing to do everything at once. They're so intent on getting where they're going, they're not enjoying the journey. Like Alberto says — when you try to see everything, you see nothing.

Don't worry about perfection. Roma wasn't built in a day — and even when it was built, it wasn't built perfectly.

Mistakes happen, in cooking and in life. Bread burns, meat spoils, sauces separate — "Così va il mondo" (so the world goes). Tomorrow we'll be cooking again.

Change is inevitable, but tradition is what gives us our identity and our strength. The old ways of doing things are often the old ways because they're the best ways. And never more so than in the kitchen. Think of the wooden spoon—a thousand years of progress has not improved on that most simple design.

The key to an easy life is flexibility—be the Italian olive tree that bends in the wind and not the English oak that snaps.

Most important of all: Listen to your Mama. Because you're not only listening to her wisdom, but the wisdom of her Mama—and her Mama before her. If everyone listened to their Mamas, the world would be a much happier, more relaxed place.

Zabaione
Zabaglione

serves 6

1/3 cup superfine sugar
6 egg yolks
3/4 cup Marsala, Madeira, or other
    sweet dessert wine
splash of brandy
amaretto cookies, to serve

Fill a saucepan halfway with water and bring to a boil. Place a heatproof bowl over the pan so that it doesn't touch the boiling water.

Put the sugar and egg yolks into the bowl and whisk until light and creamy. Add the Marsala a little at a time, whisking continuously, then add the brandy and continue whisking for up to 15 minutes, until you have a floaty, silky foam.

Pour it into bowls and serve with amaretto cookies. It can also be made ahead of time and served chilled.

Dolce di panettone
Panettone bread-and-butter pudding

serves 4-6

scant 1 cup raisins, golden
    raisins, or chopped dates
4 tbsp brandy
1¼ cups milk
scant 2 cups heavy cream
1 vanilla bean, split, or 1 tsp
    vanilla extract
scant ¾ cup butter, softened,
    plus extra for greasing
10 medium loaf-size slices of
    panettone, preferably
    chocolate-flavored, or white
    bread, crusts removed
4 eggs
¾ cup superfine sugar
vanilla ice cream, to serve

Put the raisins in a bowl with the brandy and let soften for an hour or two. In a small saucepan, warm (but don't boil) the milk and cream and add the split vanilla bean. Let stand for 30 minutes.

Preheat the oven to 350°F/180°C. Butter a shallow ovenproof dish. Butter the panettone slices, cut them diagonally in half, and lay in an overlapping pattern in the dish. Remove the softened raisins from the brandy, reserving the brandy, and sprinkle them over the panettone. In a large bowl, whisk the eggs with the sugar. Remove the vanilla bean from the milk and discard, then add the cream and milk to the egg mixture. Add the reserved brandy and whisk. Pour this mixture over the panettone and press the slices down so that they soak in the custard. Make sure that the edges don't stick out too far above the surface of the custard. Transfer to the preheated oven and bake for 30—40 minutes, until the custard has dried and set golden brown, but before the panettone burns. Serve hot, with vanilla ice cream.

Tiramisù
Tiramisu

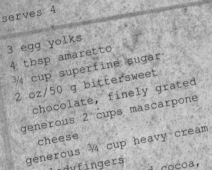

serves 4

3 egg yolks
4 tbsp amaretto
3/4 cup superfine sugar
2 oz/50 g bittersweet
  chocolate, finely grated
generous 2 cups mascarpone
  cheese
generous 3/4 cup heavy cream
24 ladyfingers
2 cups unsweetened cocoa,
  for dusting

Whisk together the egg yolks and amaretto. Gradually add the sugar and beat until the sugar has dissolved completely. Stir in the chocolate and mascarpone cheese. Whip the cream and fold it in.

Dip the unsugared side of each ladyfinger into the espresso. Arrange half the ladyfingers on the bottom of a square or rectangular dish, then cover with half the mascarpone cream.

Layer the remaining ladyfingers and cream, spreading it evenly. Cover the dish and chill overnight in the refrigerator.

Before serving, dust heavily with cocoa.

My dearest Luisa, it was so nice to spend time with you and Gianluca and the children, relaxing under the shade of the trees, enjoying the delicious food that is so abundant in our wonderful Apulian summer—washed down, of course, with some of our excellent Apulian vino!

Mama's Day Out!

Who says Mama's place is in the kitchen? Well, Alberto some days, but forget him for the moment — because when the summer sun is warm on the hills and Mama has a new hat to wear, nothing is better than a picnic!

Preparing food for a day out should not just mean the same old sandwiches. The following pages are bursting with bright, imaginative, mouthwatering ideas for the hamper. Whether it's olives with oranges and lemon, fava bean and pecorino salad, tomato tart, or dozens of other quick and easy recipes, putting on a spread all'aperto will never have been so simple — or tasted so good.

Funghi sott'olio
Mushrooms preserved in oil

serves 4

2 lb 4 oz/1 kg small mushrooms
  (button mushrooms, porcini,
  chanterelles, honey mushrooms)
1 fresh red chile
1 cup olive oil
scant ½ cup white balsamic
  vinegar
1 small sprig oregano or
  rosemary
salt

Clean the mushrooms and pat dry with paper towels.

Cut the chile in half, remove the core, and cut the flesh into fine strips.

Heat 5 tablespoons of the oil in a large skillet, add the mushrooms, and brown on all sides until the liquid has evaporated.

Add the chile to the skillet and sauté briefly. Deglaze the skillet with the vinegar, season with salt, then transfer the mushrooms to a bowl. Add the oregano and the remaining oil. Cover and let the mushrooms marinate overnight.

Red chile pepper

Porcini

Verdure miste sott'olio
Mixed vegetables in oil

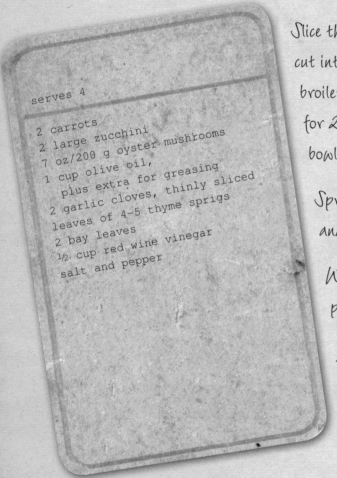

serves 4

2 carrots
2 large zucchini
7 oz/200 g oyster mushrooms
1 cup olive oil,
    plus extra for greasing
2 garlic cloves, thinly sliced
leaves of 4-5 thyme sprigs
2 bay leaves
1/2 cup red wine vinegar
salt and pepper

Slice the carrots and zucchini. Clean the mushrooms and cut into halves or quarters, depending on their size. Coat a broiler pan with olive oil and broil the vegetables in batches for 2—3 minutes on each side. Place the broiled slices in a bowl and season with salt and pepper.

Sprinkle the garlic and thyme leaves over the vegetables, and place the bay leaves in between them.

Whisk together the olive oil, vinegar, and salt and pepper and pour over the warm vegetables.

Let cool, then cover with plastic wrap and chill overnight in the refrigerator. Remove the vegetables from the refrigerator 30 minutes before serving.

Olive con arancio e limone
Olives with orange and lemon

serves 4

2 tsp fennel seeds
2 tsp cumin seeds
1¼ cups green olives
1¼ cups black olives
2 tsp grated orange rind
2 tsp grated lemon rind
3 shallots, finely chopped
pinch of ground cinnamon
¼ cup white wine vinegar
generous ¼ cup extra virgin
    olive oil
2 tbsp orange juice
1 tbsp chopped fresh mint
1 tbsp chopped fresh parsley

Dry-roast the fennel seeds and cumin seeds in a small, heavy-bottom skillet, shaking the skillet frequently, until they begin to pop and give off their aroma. Remove the skillet from the heat and let cool.

Place the olives, orange rind, lemon rind, shallots, cinnamon, and roasted seeds in a bowl.

Whisk together the vinegar, olive oil, orange juice, mint, and parsley in a bowl and pour over the olives.

Toss well, then cover and let chill for 1–2 days before serving.

Mama's essential picnic equipment

A beautiful summer day, birds soaring in the air, flowers nodding in the sunshine, the merry buzz of bees around, and adults and children eating all'aperto — what in all the world could be better than a picnic?

- Planning a picnic is about so much more than deciding what food to take. Bear in mind that once you've arrived, there can be no dashing back for anything you've forgotten. Write a list and keep it to use every summer.

- If you pack everything up to eat in the countryside as often as Mama and Alberto do, a good hamper is a necessity. Wicker is strong and light and looks the part too — but whichever you get, make sure it has straps to secure the plates, cups, and flatware as well as the food.

An old jar with some honey in it is the best way of keeping wasps away from the party. Place it a short distance away and they should leave you to enjoy your food in peace.

A picnic without wine is no picnic at all. Don't forget the corkscrew!

Even in the gentle Apulian countryside, sitting on the grass for too long has its drawbacks. Take plenty of rugs to spread out—some for food, some for people. And for those with creaking limbs like Mama, fold-out chairs are necessary too!

If you can afford (and can carry) a lightweight gazebo, they can make the difference between an ordinary lunch in the country and the kind of picnic you'll wish could last all weekend. As well as providing shade from the sun and shelter from the wind, they're a natural place for entertaining the children.

Pomodori ripiene di tonno
Tuna-stuffed tomatoes

serves 4

4 large, firm beefsteak tomatoes
5 oz/150 g canned tuna in
   oil
2 hard-cooked eggs
1 small onion,
   finely chopped
4 tbsp mayonnaise
1 tbsp finely chopped parsley
4 lettuce leaves
salt and pepper

Wash the tomatoes and cut off the tops, including the stems, for use as lids. Scoop out the cores and seeds with a spoon.

Salt the insides of the tomatoes, place upside down in a strainer, and let drain.

Drain the tuna and flake it with a fork. Peel and chop the eggs. Combine the onion, tuna, and eggs with the mayonnaise and parsley, then season with salt and pepper.

Put the filling in the tomatoes, set the tops back on, and arrange the filled tomatoes on the lettuce leaves.

Tramezzini al prosciutto e rucola
Ham and arugula sandwiches

makes 4

8 slices sandwich bread
2 tbsp mayonnaise
2 handfuls arugula
5 oz/150 g cooked ham,
   sliced
2 tomatoes, sliced
a few basil leaves
salt and pepper

Remove the crusts from the bread and spread mayonnaise on each slice. Place arugula on 4 slices, then layer with ham and tomatoes. Season with salt and pepper. Divide the basil leaves among the four sandwiches and top with the remaining bread slices. Slice each sandwich diagonally. Prosciutto, mortadella, or sliced mozzarella can be substituted for the ham.

Tramezzini al tonno
Tuna sandwiches

makes 4
7 oz/200 g canned tuna
    in oil, drained
1 tbsp capers
2 hard-cooked eggs
8 slices sandwich bread
3-4 tbsp black olive paste
8 lettuce leaves

Flake the tuna with a fork.
Finely chop the capers and
combine them with the tuna. Peel
the eggs and slice evenly. Cut
the crusts off the bread and
spread each slice with a little
of the olive paste. Divide the
tuna-caper mixture among 4 slices
of bread. Top these with sliced
egg and lettuce leaves, then
cover with the remaining slices
of bread. Cut each sandwich
diagonally.

Tramezzini ai gamberi
Shrimp sandwiches

makes 4
6 oz/175 g small shrimp,
    cooked and shelled
1 tbsp lime juice
2 hard-cooked eggs
4 tbsp mayonnaise
8 slices sandwich bread
4 lettuce leaves
salt and pepper

Season the shrimp with the
lime juice and salt and pepper.
Peel and chop the eggs. Mix the
shrimp with the eggs and
2 tablespoons of mayonnaise.
Remove the bread crusts and
spread the remaining mayonnaise
on 4 slices. Spread the shrimp
mixture on the remaining slices
and top each one with a lettuce
leaf. Cover with the mayonnaise-
spread bread slices and cut each
sandwich diagonally.

Involtini di asparagi e prosciutto
Asparagus and prosciutto wraps

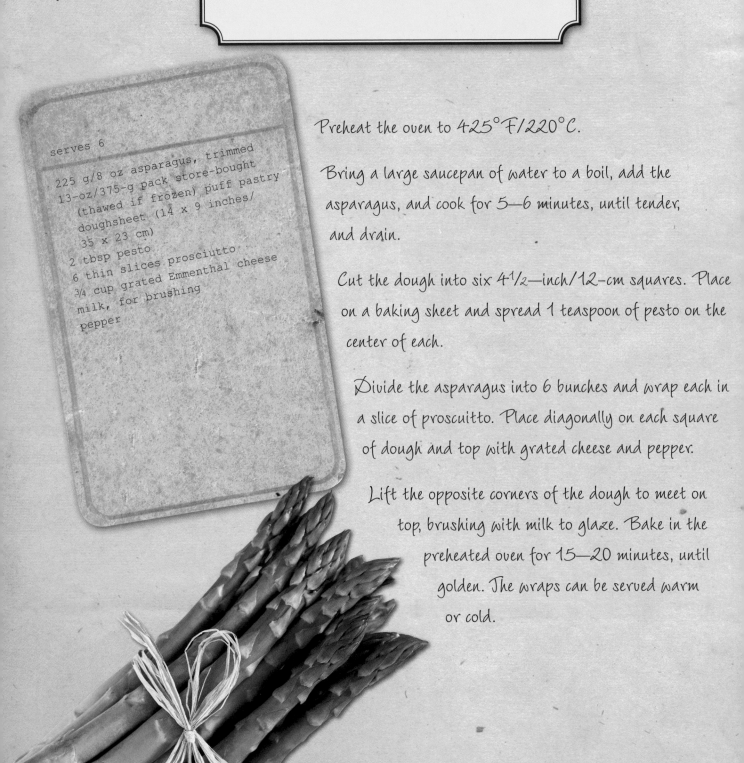

serves 6

225 g/8 oz asparagus, trimmed
13-oz/375-g pack store-bought
(thawed if frozen) puff pastry
doughsheet (14 x 9 inches/
35 x 23 cm)
2 tbsp pesto
6 thin slices prosciutto
3/4 cup grated Emmenthal cheese
milk, for brushing
pepper

Preheat the oven to 425°F/220°C.

Bring a large saucepan of water to a boil, add the asparagus, and cook for 5—6 minutes, until tender, and drain.

Cut the dough into six 4½-inch/12-cm squares. Place on a baking sheet and spread 1 teaspoon of pesto on the center of each.

Divide the asparagus into 6 bunches and wrap each in a slice of proscuitto. Place diagonally on each square of dough and top with grated cheese and pepper.

Lift the opposite corners of the dough to meet on top, brushing with milk to glaze. Bake in the preheated oven for 15—20 minutes, until golden. The wraps can be served warm or cold.

Fichi e Gorgonzola
Figs with bleu cheese

serves 4

butter, for greasing
1/2 cup superfine sugar
3/4 cup whole almonds,
  blanched or unblanched
12 ripe figs
12 oz/350 g bleu cheese,
  crumbled
extra virgin olive oil,
  for drizzling

Lightly grease a baking sheet with butter. Put the sugar in a saucepan over medium—high heat and stir until the sugar melts and turns golden brown and bubbles; do not stir once the mixture starts to bubble.

Remove from the heat and add the almonds one at a time, quickly turning with a fork until coated; if the caramel begins to harden, return the pan to the heat. Transfer each coated almond to the prepared baking sheet. Let cool until firm.

To serve, slice the figs into quarters and arrange 8 quarters on each plate. Coarsely chop the almonds by hand. Place a mound of cheese on each plate and sprinkle with chopped almonds. Drizzle the figs very lightly with oil.

Insalata di fave e pecorino
Fava bean and pecorino salad

serves 6

2 cups shelled fresh
  fava beans
5 tbsp extra virgin olive oil
2 tbsp freshly squeezed lemon
  juice
1 tbsp chopped fresh mint
6 oz/175 g young pecorino
  cheese, cut into cubes
3¼ oz/90 g arugula
2 oz/55 g aged pecorino cheese
  or Parmesan cheese, shaved
salt and pepper

If the beans are extremely fresh and tiny, you can serve them raw, but otherwise blanch them for 2—3 minutes in a large saucepan of boiling water. Drain, then rinse under cold running water and drain again.

Put the drained beans in a dish. Pour over the oil and lemon juice, then add the mint. Season well with salt and pepper and mix in the cheese cubes.

Arrange the arugula on a serving dish and spoon over the bean-and-cheese mixture. Sprinkle over the cheese shavings and serve.

Mama's Tip
If you use older beans or frozen ones, you will need 50 percent more beans to allow for the removal of the skins.

Bruschette con mozzarella
Bruschetta with mozzarella

serves 4

4 slices Tuscan country bread
2 garlic cloves
4 tbsp olive oil
5 oz/150 g buffalo
   mozzarella cheese, sliced
2 tomatoes, sliced
salt and pepper
fresh basil leaves, to garnish

Toast the bread slices on both sides, either under a broiler or in the oven, until golden brown.

Cut the garlic cloves in half. Rub each slice of bread with the cut side of a halved garlic clove, drizzle with 1 tablespoon of olive oil, then cut in half. Top the bread with sliced cheese and tomatoes, and season with salt and pepper, and garnish with basil leaves.

Toast al formaggio e pomodori secchi
Cheese and sun-dried tomato toasts

serves 4

2 sfilatini or baguettes
¾ cup sun-dried tomato paste
10½ oz/300 g mozzarella cheese,
    drained and diced
1¼ tsp dried oregano
2-3 tbsp olive oil
pepper

Preheat the oven to 425°F/220°C.

Slice the loaves diagonally and discard the end pieces. Toast the slices on both sides under a preheated broiler until golden.

Spread one side of each toast with the sun-dried tomato paste and top with cheese. Sprinkle with oregano and season with pepper.

Place the toasts on a large baking sheet and drizzle with olive oil. Bake in the preheated oven for about 5 minutes, until the cheese has melted and is bubbling. Remove the hot toasts from the oven and let stand for 5 minutes before serving.

Sgonfiotti al formaggio
Fried cheese pastries

makes about 25

scant 1½ cups all-purpose flour,
    plus extra for dusting
2 eggs, lightly beaten
2 tbsp olive oil
1-2 tbsp cold water
1 egg white, beaten until
    slightly frothy
salt
vegetable oil, for deep-frying

filling
generous ½ cup ricotta cheese
1 egg, lightly beaten
2½ oz/70 g mozzarella cheese,
    finely diced
1 oz/25 g Parmesan cheese,
    finely diced
1½ oz/40 g salami or Parma ham,
    finely chopped
1 tbsp chopped fresh flat-leaf
    parsley
salt and pepper

To make the filling, mix together all the ingredients in a bowl and season. Sift the flour into a large bowl. Make a well in the center and pour in the eggs. Add the oil and a pinch of salt. Stir with a fork, gradually drawing in the flour from around the edge. Once a dough has formed, knead for about 10 minutes, until smooth and silky. Wrap the dough in plastic wrap and let rest in the refrigerator for at least 30 minutes or overnight.

Roll out the dough very thinly and, using a pastry cutter, stamp out circles about 2¾ inches/7 cm in diameter, revolling the dough until it is all used. Place the circles on a clean dish towel. Wet the edges of the circles with egg white. Place a teaspoon of filling in the middle, then fold over one half of the dough to form a semicircle. Press the edges together, making sure they stick. Let rest on the dish towel for 30 minutes.

Heat the vegetable oil in a deep-fat fryer or large saucepan to 350°F/180°C, or until a cube of bread browns in 30 seconds. Drop the pastries into the hot oil, a few at a time, deep-frying for 3—5 minutes. Remove from the pan and drain on crumpled paper towels. Serve at once, while still hot.

Torta di pomodori
Tomato tart

serves 4

2 tbsp butter
1 tbsp superfine sugar
1 lb 2 oz/500 g cherry tomatoes,
   halved
1 clove garlic, crushed
2 tsp white wine vinegar
salt and pepper
chopped oregano, to garnish

crust
scant 1 cup all-purpose flour
pinch of salt
1 tbsp chopped oregano
generous ½ cup butter
5-6 tbsp cold water

Preheat the oven to 400°F/200°C. Melt the butter in a heavy-bottom saucepan. Add the sugar and stir over fairly high heat until just turning golden brown.

Remove from the heat and quickly add the tomatoes, garlic, and vinegar, stirring to coat evenly. Season with salt and pepper.

Tip the tomatoes into a 9-inch/23-cm round cake pan, spreading evenly.

For the crust, place the flour, salt, oregano, and butter in a food processor and process to fine crumbs. Add just enough water to bind to a soft, but not sticky, dough. Roll out to a 10-inch/25-cm circle and place over the tomatoes, tucking in the edges. Pierce with a fork to let out the steam.

Bake in the preheated oven for 25—30 minutes, until firm and golden. Let rest for 2—3 minutes, then run a knife around the edge and turn out onto a warmed serving plate to garnish with the oregano.

Mama's Tip
Serve the tart warm,
sprinkled with chopped
oregano, with an arugula
or baby spinach salad.

Crostini
Topped toasts

Crostini neri
Crostini with olive paste

makes 12
generous 1 cup pitted black
  olives
3 anchovy fillets in oil
1 tbsp capers
3-4 tbsp olive oil
12 small slices Tuscan
  white bread or ciabatta
12 basil leaves
salt
cayenne pepper

Coarsely chop the olives
and anchovy fillets, then
puree them together with
the capers and as much
oil as is needed to make a
thick paste. Season with
salt and cayenne pepper.

Toast the bread on both
sides under a broiler or
in the oven until golden
brown. Spread each slice
with olive paste and
garnish with a basil leaf.

Crostini con erbe e pomodori
Crostini with herbs and tomatoes

makes 12
6 plum tomatoes
1 small bunch basil
2 garlic cloves, minced
3 tbsp olive oil
1 tbsp finely chopped
  parsley
½ tsp finely chopped oregano
12 small slices Tuscan
  white bread or ciabatta
salt and pepper

Peel the tomatoes, quarter,
core, and cut into small
dice. Cut the basil leaves
into fine strips. Combine
the tomatoes with the
garlic, oil, salt and
pepper, and herbs and let
stand briefly.

Toast the bread on both
sides under a broiler or in
the oven until golden brown.
Top each slice with some of
the tomato mixture.

Crostini alla Toscana
Crostini with chicken liver pâté

makes 12
7 oz/200 g chicken livers
2 tbsp olive oil
1 shallot, finely chopped
scant ½ cup Vin Santo
1 tbsp finely chopped thyme
12 small slices of Tuscan
  white bread or ciabatta
salt and pepper

Rinse and dry the livers,
remove the membranes, and
chop into small pieces.

Heat the oil in a large
skillet, add the shallot,
and sauté until translucent.
Add the livers and sauté.
Deglaze the skillet with
the wine, add the thyme,
and cook until the wine has
almost evaporated. Remove
from the heat, let cool
slightly, then puree. Season
with salt and pepper.

Toast the bread on both
sides under a broiler or in
the oven until golden brown.
Let cool slightly, then
spread with the pâté and
serve immediately.

Crostini al pomodoro
Crostini with tomatoes

makes 12
12 small slices Tuscan
  white bread or ciabatta
2 garlic cloves
2-3 tbsp olive oil
4 small beefsteak tomatoes,
  sliced
1¾ oz/50 g Parmesan cheese
salt and pepper
a few basil leaves,
  to garnish

Toast the bread on both
sides under a broiler or in
the oven until golden brown.
Peel the garlic cloves and
cut them in half. Rub the
toasted bread with garlic
and drizzle with oil. Top
with tomato slices, season
with salt and pepper, and
thinly grate the cheese over
the tomatoes.

Garnish with basil leaves
cut into fine strips.

Prosciutto con la rucola
Prosciutto with arugula

serves 4

4 oz/115 g arugula
1 tbsp lemon juice
3 tbsp extra virgin olive oil
8 oz/225 g prosciutto, sliced
   thinly
salt and pepper

Place the arugula in a bowl. Pour the lemon juice into a small bowl and season with salt and pepper. Whisk in the olive oil, then pour the dressing over the arugula leaves and toss lightly so they are evenly coated.

Carefully drape the prosciutto in folds on 4 individual serving plates, then add the arugula.

Serve at room temperature.

Risi e bisi
Rice and peas

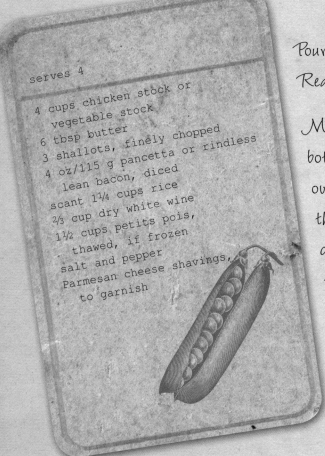

serves 4

4 cups chicken stock or
  vegetable stock
6 tbsp butter
3 shallots, finely chopped
4 oz/115 g pancetta or rindless
  lean bacon, diced
scant 1¼ cups rice
⅔ cup dry white wine
1½ cups petits pois,
  thawed, if frozen
salt and pepper
Parmesan cheese shavings,
  to garnish

Pour the stock into a large saucepan and bring to a boil. Reduce the heat and let simmer gently.

Melt 4 tablespoons of the butter in a large, heavy-bottom saucepan. Add the shallots and pancetta and cook over low heat, stirring occasionally, for 5 minutes, until the shallots are softened. Add the rice and cook, stirring continuously, for 2—3 minutes, until all the grains are thoroughly coated and glistening.

Pour in the wine and cook, stirring continuously, until it has almost completely evaporated. Add a ladleful of hot stock and cook, stirring continuously, until all the stock has been absorbed. Continue cooking and adding the stock, a ladleful at a time, for about 10 minutes.

Add the peas, then continue adding the stock, a ladleful at a time, for an additional 10 minutes, or until the rice is tender and the liquid has been absorbed. Stir in the remaining butter and season with salt and pepper. Transfer to a warmed serving dish, garnish with cheese shavings, and serve immediately.

Mama's tips on keeping the kids entertained

Every year all of Mama's family get together for a picnic. At the last count there were 38 of us, from six months to more than 80 years of age! Making sure that there is enough food for everyone is hard work. Such a day out also means a lot of preparation has to go in to keeping the little ones happy.

In Apulia we say, "Nelle botti piccine ci sta il vino buono": you find the good wine in the small barrels. Children bring joy to any occasion. They should not be sidelined to fit in with the adults' plans, but celebrated as the center around which the whole day out revolves.

Children never stop running. Use that energy to let them work up an appetite: Frisbees, footballs, and tennis rackets are all essential. Last summer my sons Marco and Filippo organized all the children into teams for a game they made up as they went along, a cross between touch rugby and American football, played with a Frisbee. It was a great success — and if they can remember the rules, it's sure to be played again this year.

Of course, there is one sure way to keep any child entertained—good food and plenty of it!

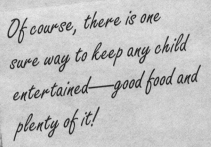

For those who are too little to join in the sport, a sing-along and even a dance will help keep them happy.

My daughter Maria's husband always brings fishing poles for the bigger children and nets for the little ones. Every year they swear they'll catch something for supper—and every year Mama has to inspect the minnows in the jelly jars, consider carefully, and announce that if we put them back, then maybe they'll be big enough to eat next year.

Don't forget the old games. Mama used to play hide-and-seek in the olive groves here back before the war even—and I still smile when I see the children today running to hide in the same places I did as a little girl.

Biscotti/cantucci di mandorle
Almond biscotti

makes 20-30

1²/₃ cups whole blanched almonds
scant 1½ cups all-purpose flour,
    plus 1 tbsp for dusting
scant 1 cup superfine sugar,
    plus 1 tbsp for sprinkling
1 tsp baking powder
½ tsp ground cinnamon
2 eggs
2 tsp vanilla extract

Preheat the oven to 350°F/180°C. Line two cookie sheets with parchment paper.

Very coarsely chop the almonds, leaving some whole. Mix the flour, sugar, baking powder, and cinnamon together in a mixing bowl. Stir in all the almonds.

Beat the eggs with the vanilla extract in a small bowl, then add to the flour mixture and mix together to form a firm dough.

Turn out the dough onto a lightly floured counter and knead lightly. Divide the dough in half and shape each piece into a long, thick log, roughly 2 inches/5 cm wide. Transfer to the prepared cookie sheets and sprinkle with sugar, then bake in the preheated oven for 20—25 minutes, or until brown and firm. Remove from the oven and let cool for a few minutes, then transfer the logs to a cutting board and cut into ½-inch/1-cm slices. Meanwhile, reduce the oven temperature to 325°F/160°C. Arrange the cookies, cut-side down, on the cookie sheets. Bake in the oven for 15—20 minutes, or until dry and crisp. Remove from the oven and let cool on a wire rack. Store in an airtight container to keep crisp.

Mama's Tip
Almonds are traditional, but you can make these biscotti with any other nuts, such as walnuts or pistachios.

Torta al cioccolato
Soft chocolate cake

serves 6-8

generous ½ cup unsalted butter,
    plus extra for greasing
10 oz/280 g semisweet chocolate
    with at least 72% cocoa
    solids, broken into pieces
4 eggs, separated
¼ cup superfine sugar
generous 2 tbsp all-purpose
    flour
1 tsp vanilla extract
unsweetened cocoa, for dusting

Preheat the oven to 350°F/180°C. Grease and line the bottom of an 8-inch/20-cm springform cake pan with a removable bottom. Put the chocolate and butter in a heatproof bowl, then set the bowl over a saucepan of barely simmering water and heat until melted. Remove the bowl from the heat and let cool for 5 minutes. Whisk the eggs yolks and sugar together in a mixing bowl with a handheld electric mixer or a hand whisk until thick and creamy. In a separate mixing bowl, whisk the egg whites until thick and glossy. Fold the egg yolk mixture into the melted chocolate. Sift in the flour and fold in together with the vanilla extract. Gently fold in the beaten egg whites.

Turn the mixture into the prepared pan and bake in the preheated oven for 15—20 minutes. Do not overcook. The top should be firm but the center still slightly gooey. Remove from the oven and let cool, covered, overnight.

Remove the cake pan and peel away the lining paper from the bottom. Dust the surface of the cake with cocoa and serve in slices.

Cenci
Deep-fried pie dough ribbons

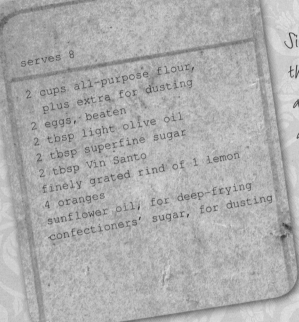

serves 8

2 cups all-purpose flour,
    plus extra for dusting
2 eggs, beaten
2 tbsp light olive oil
2 tbsp superfine sugar
2 tbsp Vin Santo
finely grated rind of 1 lemon
4 oranges
sunflower oil, for deep-frying
confectioners' sugar, for dusting

Sift the flour into a large mixing bowl and make a well in the center. Add the eggs, the olive oil, sugar, Vin Santo, and lemon rind. Mix together with a palette knife to form a dough. Use your hands to knead until smooth. Form into a ball, then wrap in plastic wrap and chill in the refrigerator for 1 hour. Meanwhile, working over a bowl to catch the juice, peel and segment the oranges with a sharp knife. Add the segments to the juice, then cover and chill in the refrigerator until required. Divide the dough in half and roll out one half on a lightly floured counter to a rectangle about 1/8 inch/3 mm thick.

Cover and repeat with the remaining dough. Using a fluted pastry cutting wheel, cut the dough into 4 x 1-inch/ 10 x 2.5-cm ribbons. Tie a single knot in each ribbon. Alternatively, cut the dough into diamond shapes and leave flat. Heat the oil for deep-frying in a deep-fat fryer or large saucepan to 350°F/180°C, or until a cube of bread browns in 30 seconds.

Add the dough ribbons, in small batches, and cook until golden brown. Remove with a slotted spoon and drain on paper towels, then keep warm while you cook the remaining dough ribbons. Dust with confectioners' sugar before serving warm with the orange segments.

Mama's Tip
Sliced ripe apricots and peaches can be used instead of oranges. Marinate in 3 tablespoons of Vin Santo.

My dear Luisa, I am so pleased to hear you had success with the ciabatta recipe!

Mama's Baking Day

Where would we be without baking? Everyone knows Italians make the best bread in the world, and everyone in this part of Apulia knows Mama makes the best in Italy. Included here are no less than seven bread recipes, including ciabatta, focaccia with sage, and a pesto and olive soda bread that Alberto swears tastes better than anything in all of Italy.

As if that wasn't enough, there are galettes, pastries, tarts, pies, Stromboli, brioche, and Mama's favorite bad habit — almond biscotti.

Baking need not be as difficile as they say. Follow Mama's advice and baking day will be a day of both comfort and self-indulgence.

Pane casalingo di oliva
Homemade olive bread

makes 3 small loaves

3½ cups flour,
  plus extra for dusting
1 envelope active dry yeast
1 tsp salt
1 pinch of sugar
1¼ cups lukewarm water
2 tbsp olive oil, plus extra
  for greasing
¾ cup chopped, pitted black
  olives
9 oz/250 g Swiss chard,
  chopped

Sift the flour into a bowl and make a hollow in the middle. Place the yeast, salt, and sugar in the hollow, then add the water. Knead the mixture into a smooth, silky dough. Let rise, covered, for about 1 hour, or until it has doubled in size.

Preheat the oven to 425°F/220°C and grease a baking sheet. Knead the Swiss chard and olives into the dough, then divide it into thirds.

Form each third into a rounded rectangular loaf and place on a greased baking sheet. Cover with a flour-dusted dish towel and let rise again for 1 hour.

Brush the loaves with oil and bake in the preheated oven for 20—25 minutes. Let cool thoroughly on a wire rack.

Focaccia con cipolle
Flatbread with onions

makes 1 loaf

2 envelopes active dry yeast
1 cup lukewarm water
1 pinch of sugar
3 cups white bread flour, plus
   extra for dusting
1 tsp salt
1/2 cup olive oil,
   plus extra for greasing
2 onions, cut into thin rings
3/4 cup pitted black olives
2-3 garlic cloves, finely chopped
1 tbsp coarse sea salt
2 tsp crushed peppercorns

Crumble the yeast into the lukewarm water, add the sugar, and dissolve.

Stir in 4 tablespoons of the flour, cover, and let rise in a warm place for 15 minutes.

Sift the remaining flour into a bowl, make a hollow in the center, and pour the yeast mixture into it. Add the salt and 3—4 tablespoons of olive oil and knead into a silky dough. Shape it into a ball, cover, and set in a warm spot to rise for 1 hour, or until doubled in volume.

Grease a baking sheet with oil and preheat the oven to 475°F/240°C.

Vigorously knead the dough again. On a floured counter, roll out the dough to a thickness of about 3/4 inch/2 cm, then place on the baking sheet and prick with a fork. Cover with the onions and olives and sprinkle with garlic. Drizzle over the remaining olive oil, season with sea salt and crushed peppercorns, and bake in the preheated oven for about 20 minutes.

Ciabatta

Ciabatta

First, make the biga. Sift the flour into a bowl, stir in the yeast, and make a well in the center. Pour in the water and stir until the dough comes together. Turn out onto a lightly floured counter and knead for 5 minutes, until smooth and elastic. Shape the dough into a ball, put it into a bowl, and put the bowl into a plastic bag or cover with a damp dish towel. Let rise in a warm place for 12 hours, until just beginning to collapse.

Gradually mix the water and milk into the biga, beating with a wooden spoon. Gradually mix in the flour and yeast with your hands, adding them a little at a time. Finally, mix in the salt and oil with your hands. The dough will be very wet; do not add extra flour. Put the bowl into a plastic bag or cover with a damp dish towel and let the dough rise in a warm place for 2 hours, until doubled in volume.

Dust 3 cookie sheets with flour. Using a spatula, divide the dough among the prepared cookie sheets without knocking out the air. With lightly floured hands, gently pull and shape each piece of dough into a rectangular loaf, then flatten slightly. Dust the tops of the loaves with flour and let rise in a warm place for 30 minutes.

Meanwhile, preheat the oven to 425°F/220°C. Bake the loaves in the preheated oven for 25—30 minutes, until the crust is lightly golden and the loaves sound hollow when tapped on the bottom with your knuckles. Transfer to wire racks to cool.

We bring ciabatta and salt whenever we're invited to a house-warming party!

makes 3 loaves

1¾ cups lukewarm water
4 tbsp lukewarm low-fat milk
4½ cups white bread flour
1 envelope active dry yeast
2 tsp salt
3 tbsp olive oil

biga
3 cups white bread flour,
   plus extra for dusting
1¼ tsp active dry yeast
scant 1 cup lukewarm water

Mama's essential baking equipment

Some say that if cooking is an art, then baking is a science. Whereas with a stew or a sauce or a salad you can improvise and experiment, with baking you have to be strict. Stick to the measurements, follow the recipe carefully, or poof! Disastro! And that means that having the right equipment is vital.

One of the most common mistakes made when baking is forgetting the importance of letting things cool properly. I keep a stack of wire racks and have a space near the window for my baking to stand after it comes out of the oven. Not only does this let the cooking process finish properly, it fills the house and yard with the beautiful aroma of freshly baked bread!

My rolling pin belonged to my Mama's Mama. It's already promised to my Maria's daughter Fiorella.
It's nothing to look at—but this long, old wooden pin has helped three generations of women in my family feed their loved ones.

Measuring spoons and cups should also be well-maintained. I keep two sets: one dry, one wet.

You need two kinds of spatula. A metal one with the thinnest edge you can find is a must, and I now use a rubber one too. It was a Christmas present from my great-grand-daughter Elena and I use it for folding.

Lastly, a set of ice-cream scoops — in the old spring-loaded style — makes scooping things into perfect balls so much easier than doing it by hand. Just remember to keep one aside for the gelato itself!

Pane Toscano
Tuscan unsalted bread

makes 1 large or 2 smaller loaves

3½ cups white bread flour,
  plus extra for dusting
1½ tsp active dry yeast
2 tbsp olive oil, plus extra
  for oiling
1¼ cups lukewarm water

Mix the flour and yeast together in a mixing bowl.

Make a well in the center. Mix together the olive oil and water in a pitcher and pour into the well. Gradually mix the liquid into the flour mixture with a palette knife. Gather the mixture together with your hands to form a soft dough.

Turn out the dough onto a lightly floured counter and knead for 5—7 minutes, or until very smooth and elastic. Return the dough to the bowl and cover with a clean dish towel or oiled plastic wrap, then let rise in a warm place for 1 hour, or until doubled in size. Turn out and gently knead again for 1 minute, or until smooth.

Preheat the oven to 400°F/200°C. Oil 1 or 2 cookie sheets. Shape the dough into 1 large oval or 2 smaller ovals and transfer to the prepared cookie sheet or sheets. Cover with a clean dish towel or oiled plastic wrap and let rise in a warm place for 30 minutes. Make several slashes in the top of the bread with a sharp knife. Bake in the preheated oven for 30—35 minutes (or 20—25 minutes for 2 loaves). If the bread is getting too brown, reduce the temperature a little. To test that the bread is cooked, turn it over and tap it on the bottom — it should sound hollow. Let cool on a wire rack.

Mama's Tip
The Tuscans like to eat salty, spicy food such as sausages. This traditional unsalted bread is an ideal accompaniment to their highly seasoned food.

Focaccia con cipolle e rosmarino
Flatbread with onion and rosemary

Mix together the flour, yeast, and salt in a mixing bowl, then stir in the chopped rosemary. Make a well in the center.

Mix 3 tablespoons of the oil with the water in a pitcher and pour into the well. Gradually mix the liquid into the flour mixture with a palette knife. Gather the mixture together with your hands to form a soft dough.

Turn out the dough onto a lightly floured counter and knead for 8—10 minutes, or until very smooth and elastic. Return the dough to the bowl and cover with a clean dish towel or oiled plastic wrap, then let rise in a warm place for 45—60 minutes, or until doubled in size. Turn out and gently knead again for 1 minute, or until smooth.

Preheat the oven to 400°F/200°C. Oil a cookie sheet. Gently roll out the dough to a circle about 12 inches/30 cm in diameter. It doesn't have to be a perfect circle; a slightly oval shape is traditional. Transfer to the prepared cookie sheet and cover with a clean dish towel or oiled

Mama's Tip

Sun-dried tomatoes and chopped olives can be added before the final rising or just sprinkled on top for extra flavor.

makes 1 loaf

3½ cups white bread flour,
    plus extra for dusting
1½ tsp active dry yeast
½ tsp salt
2 tbsp chopped fresh rosemary,
    plus extra small sprigs to
    garnish
5 tbsp extra virgin olive oil,
    plus extra for oiling
1¼ cups lukewarm water
1 red onion, finely sliced and
    separated into rings
1 tbsp coarse sea salt,
    for sprinkling

plastic wrap, then let rise in a warm place for
20—30 minutes.

Make holes about 2 inches/5 cm apart all over
the surface of the dough with the handle of a wooden
spoon. Spread the onion rings over the dough, then
drizzle with the remaining oil and sprinkle over the
sea salt. Bake in the preheated oven for 20—25 minutes, or
until well risen and golden brown. Five minutes before the end of
the cooking time, garnish with the rosemary sprigs. Transfer to a
wire rack to cool for a few minutes, then serve the bread warm.

Pane con pesto ed olive
Pesto and olive soda bread

makes 1 loaf

olive oil, for greasing
2¼ cups all-purpose flour
2¼ cups whole-wheat flour
1 tsp baking soda
½ tsp salt
3 tbsp pesto
1¼ cups buttermilk
½ cup coarsely chopped, pitted
  green olives
milk, to glaze

Preheat the oven to 400°F/200°C and grease a baking sheet. Sift the flours, baking soda, and salt into a bowl, adding back any bran from the sifter.

Combine the pesto and buttermilk. Stir into the flour with the olives, mixing to a soft dough. Add more liquid if needed.

Shape the dough into an 8-inch/20-cm circle and place on the baking sheet. Flatten slightly and cut a deep cross in the top with a sharp knife.

Brush with milk and bake for 30—35 minutes, until golden brown. The loaf should sound hollow when tapped on the bottom. Serve on the day of baking, with soup or cheese and salad for a healthy lunch.

Polenta Parmigiana
Parmesan polenta

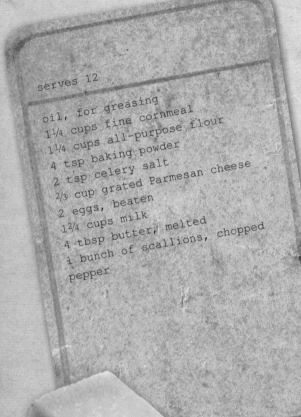

serves 12

oil, for greasing
1¼ cups fine cornmeal
1¼ cups all-purpose flour
4 tsp baking powder
2 tsp celery salt
2/3 cup grated Parmesan cheese
2 eggs, beaten
1²/4 cups milk
4 tbsp butter, melted
1 bunch of scallions, chopped
pepper

Parmesan Cheese

Preheat the oven to 375°F/190°C. Grease a 9-inch/ 23-cm square baking pan.

Sift the cornmeal, flour, baking powder, celery salt, and a pinch of pepper into a bowl and stir in ½ cup of the cheese. Beat together the eggs, milk, and melted butter.

Add the egg mixture to the dry ingredients and stir well to mix evenly. Stir in the chopped scallions and spread the mixture evenly into the pan.

Sprinkle the remaining cheese over the mixture. Bake in the preheated oven for 30—35 minutes, or until firm and golden.

Mama's Tip

Plump juicy figs, caramelized almonds, and piquant bleu cheese are a mouthwatering alternative. Try robust and spicy Gorgonzola piccante or the milder dolcelatte, both from Lombardy in northern Italy.

Torta di broccoli, pancetta e Gorgonzola
Broccoli, pancetta, and bleu cheese galette

serves 4

1 sheet store-bought frozen puff
  pastry dough, thawed
  (11 x 8½ inches/28 x 21.5 cm)
3 cups small broccoli
  florets, halved if necessary
3½ oz/100 g diced pancetta
1 small red onion, sliced
3½ oz/100 g Gorgonzola or
  other bleu cheese, chopped
pepper
toasted pine nuts, to garnish

Preheat the oven to 400°C/200°C. Place the pastry on a baking sheet and lightly score a line all around, cutting only halfway through, about ½ inch/1 cm from the edge

Steam or boil the broccoli for 4–5 minutes, until just tender. Drain.

Fry the pancetta with the onion, stirring, until golden. Stir in the broccoli and season with pepper.

Spread the broccoli mixture over the pastry, leaving the border clear.

Scatter the pieces of cheese evenly over the top. Bake the galette in the preheated oven for 25–30 minutes, until the pastry is risen and golden. Garnish with pine nuts and serve.

Gorgonzola Dolce

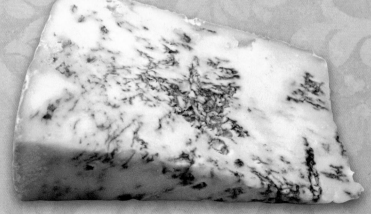

Mama's Tip
Sprinkle with
toasted pine
nuts and serve
warm, with a
tomato salad.

Caprino in crosta
Goat cheese in pastry

serves 4

- 1 envelope active dry yeast
- 1 pinch of sugar
- 7 tbsp lukewarm water
- 1½ cups white bread flour, plus extra for dusting
- ½ tsp salt
- 2 tbsp olive oil, plus extra for greasing
- 1 tsp finely chopped oregano
- 10½ oz/300 g fresh goat cheese (log)
- 1 egg, separated

Dissolve the yeast and sugar in the lukewarm water. Sift the flour into a bowl and make a well in the middle. Add the salt, olive oil, and yeast–water mixture and knead everything into a smooth, silky dough. Form the dough into a ball, cover with a clean dish towel or oiled plastic wrap, and let rise in a warm place for an hour, or until doubled in size.

Preheat the oven to 390°F/200°C and grease a baking sheet. Vigorously knead the dough once more, working in the oregano, then roll it out on a floured counter.

Cut the cheese into slices of equal thickness. Cut out 8 dough circles slightly larger than the cheese slices. Place a slice of cheese on 4 of the dough circles and brush the edges of the dough with egg white. Cover with the remaining dough circles and press the edges together firmly. Place the filled pockets on the baking sheet and brush with whisked egg yolk. Bake in the preheated oven for about 20 minutes.

Torta di pomodori e formaggio
Cheese and tomato tart

serves 4

scant 1 cup white bread flour
scant 1 cup self-rising flour
generous 1/2 cup chilled butter,
    diced
1 egg yolk
4 tbsp cold water
salt
oil, for greasing

filling
8-9 tomatoes, peeled, seeded,
    and cut into eighths
1¼ cups coarsely grated
    Emmenthal cheese
4 eggs
generous 1/3 cup heavy cream
2 tbsp chopped fresh oregano or
    marjoram
1 tbsp chopped fresh chives
salt and pepper

Sift the flours and salt into a bowl, then sift again. Work the butter into the flours, rubbing between your fingertips until the mixture resembles fine breadcrumbs. Beat together the egg yolk and water and stir into the flour mixture with a fork. Once the dough starts to clump, knead very lightly to form a compact ball. Wrap in plastic wrap and let chill in the refrigerator for at least 30 minutes.

Preheat the oven to 325°F/160°C. Lightly grease an 11-inch/28-cm loose-bottom tart pan. Roll out the dough very thinly and use to line the pan. Using the side of your index finger, press the dough into the corner of the pan to raise it slightly above the rim. Line the pastry shell with wax paper and weigh down with dried beans. Bake in the preheated oven for 15 minutes.

Arrange the tomato segments in the pastry shell in concentric circles. Sprinkle the grated cheese evenly over the top. Beat the eggs lightly, then stir in the cream, oregano, chives, and salt and pepper. Mix well, then pour into the pastry shell. Return to the oven and bake for 20—25 minutes, until puffed and golden. Serve hot or warm.

Torta verde
Spinach pie

serves 6-8

2 cups all-purpose flour,
  plus extra for dusting
5 tbsp olive oil, plus extra
  for greasing and brushing
pinch of salt
2-4 tbsp water
3 lb 5 oz/1.5 kg leaf spinach
1 onion, finely chopped
1 garlic clove, finely chopped
5 eggs
scant 1 cup grated Parmesan cheese
1 egg yolk
salt and pepper

Sift the flour onto a counter and make a well in the center.
Put 2 tablespoons of the olive oil and the salt and water
into the well and knead everything into a smooth, supple
dough.

Form the dough into a ball, cover it in plastic wrap,
and let chill for 30 minutes in the refrigerator.

Bring a large saucepan of lightly salted water to
a boil. Thoroughly wash the spinach, removing any
wilted leaves and coarse stems. Plunge it into the
boiling water and blanch it briefly. Pour off the hot
water and refresh the spinach in cold water. Drain,
then finely chop the spinach. Preheat the oven to
400°F/200°C and grease a 10-inch/26-cm round
springform cake pan.

Heat the remaining olive oil in a saucepan, add the onion and
garlic, and sauté briefly. Add the spinach, season with salt and
pepper, and sauté a few minutes longer, stirring continuously.
Remove from the heat and let cool. Whisk the eggs, stir
in the cheese, and combine with the spinach. Roll out the

dough on a floured counter. Cut out two circles of dough the size of the bottom of the springform pan. Lay one circle on the bottom of the pan and use scraps of dough to form a border up the side. Spread the spinach mixture over the bottom, smoothing the surface, and lay the second dough circle on top.

Prick several holes in the top with a fork. Fold over the sides of the dough and press together firmly. Decorate with the remaining dough, if desired, and brush the surface with the egg yolk. Bake in the preheated oven for about 1 hour. Serve hot or cold.

Stromboli
Savory roulade

makes 1 loaf

4½ cups white bread flour
2½ tsp active dry yeast
2 tsp sea salt flakes
3 tbsp olive oil, plus extra
    for greasing
1½ cups lukewarm water

filling
3 oz/85 g thinly sliced
    Italian salami
1½ cups diced mozzarella cheese
½ cup basil leaves
2 red bell peppers, roasted,
    peeled, seeded, and sliced
pepper

Combine the flour, yeast, and 1½ teaspoons of the salt, then stir in the oil with enough water to make a soft dough.

Turn out the dough onto a floured counter and knead for about 10 minutes. Cover with a clean dish towel or oiled plastic wrap, and set aside in a warm place for 1 hour, until doubled in size.

Knead lightly for 2—3 minutes, until smooth. Cover and let stand for an additional 10 minutes.

Roll out the dough to a rectangle about 15 x 10 inches/38 x 25 cm, and ½ inch/1 cm thick.

Preheat the oven to 425°F/220°C. Grease a baking sheet. Spread the salami over the dough and top with the cheese, basil, and bell peppers. Season with pepper.

Roll up firmly from the long side, pinch the ends, and put onto the prepared baking sheet, with the seam underneath. Cover and let stand for 10 minutes.

Pierce the roll deeply several times with a skewer. Brush with oil and sprinkle with the remaining salt. Bake in the preheated oven for 30—35 minutes, or until firm and golden. Let cool on a wire rack. Serve fresh and warm, cut into thick slices.

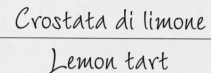

Crostata di limone
Lemon tart

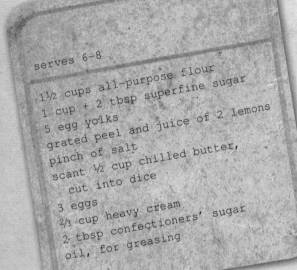

serves 6–8

- 1½ cups all-purpose flour
- 1 cup + 2 tbsp superfine sugar
- 5 egg yolks
- grated peel and juice of 2 lemons
- pinch of salt
- scant ½ cup chilled butter, cut into dice
- 3 eggs
- 2/3 cup heavy cream
- 2 tbsp confectioners' sugar
- oil, for greasing

Sift the flour onto a counter, blend in 7 tablespoons of sugar, and make a well in the center. Add 4 egg yolks, half the lemon peel, the salt, and the butter. Knead everything into a smooth, supple dough. Form the dough into a ball, cover it in plastic wrap, and chill for 1 hour in the refrigerator.

Preheat the oven to 350°F/180°C and grease a 10-inch/26-cm round springform tart pan. On a floured counter, roll out the dough very thinly and use to line the bottom and sides of the pan. Use a fork to prick several holes in the dough, then lay a sheet of parchment paper over it. Fill with dried beans and bake for 15 minutes. Remove the dried beans and parchment paper and let the shell cool.

Preheat the oven to 350°F/180°C. Beat the remaining egg yolk, the whole eggs, and the rest of the sugar and lemon peel into a thick, pale cream. Stir in the lemon juice. Whip the cream and fold it into the egg mixture. Pour it into the shell and spread evenly, then bake in the preheated oven for 20 minutes. Dust the surface with confectioners' sugar, then return the tart to the oven until golden brown.

Brioche ai cioccolato e zafferano
Chocolate and saffron brioches

makes 12

pinch of saffron threads
3 tbsp boiling water
4 tbsp butter, melted
2¼ cups all-purpose flour
pinch of salt
1 tbsp superfine sugar
2½ tsp active dry yeast
2 eggs, beaten
6 squares bittersweet chocolate,
    halved, 1 oz/30 g in total
milk, for glazing

Add the saffron to the boiling water and let cool completely.

Lightly brush 12 individual brioche pans or fluted patty pans with butter.

Sift the flour, salt, and sugar together and stir in the yeast. Add the saffron liquid, eggs, and remaining butter to make a soft dough.

Knead until smooth, then cover and let rise in a warm place for 1—1½ hours, until doubled in size. Knead briefly, then shape three quarters of the dough into 12 balls. Place one in every pan and press a piece of chocolate firmly into each.

Shape the remaining dough into 12 small balls, each with a pointed end. Brush with milk and press the balls into each brioche, sealing well.

Cover with oiled plastic wrap and let stand in a warm place for 1½ hours, or until doubled in size.

Meanwhile, preheat the oven to 400°F/200°C. Brush the brioches with milk and bake for 12—15 minutes, until firm and golden. Turn out and serve warm, for breakfast or with coffee.

Mama's tips for successful baking

A kitchen without fresh baking is like a house without laughter. You probably thought that baking your own ciabatta, focaccia, olive bread, or pastry would be difficult, but Mama has shown you how easy it can be.

- As I said before, baking is more scienza than arte. Save self-expression for the finishing touches — for everything else, follow Mama to the letter. If the recipe calls for an 8-inch/20-cm pan, then a 7-inch/18-cm pan will not work!

- Remember why you're baking.

- Kitchens should not be a place for stress and worry. You're baking because you want to, because the smell and taste of fresh ciabatta is worth any difficulties in the recipe. Mama didn't get it right every time when she started either!

Mama's Tip

Don't be tempted to overbake. If anything, remove things from the oven a little early, because the heat inside will keep them cooking even as they cool.

Always melt butter at low temperatures to avoid burning.

Don't be tempted to keep checking on your baking. Once things are in the oven, let them be. Opening the door lets out heat and will affect how things are cooked.

Mama's trick for measuring sticky stuff such as honey or melted chocolate: Use the same cup that you used for measuring your oil. That way your honey will pour out without some of it sticking and being left behind.

Remember: After the dough cleans the bowl and forms a ball on one side, do not add any more flour!

Biscotti ai mirtilli e pinoli
Cranberry and pine nut biscotti

makes 18-20

butter or oil, for greasing
scant ½ cup dark brown sugar
1 extra-large egg
1¼ cups all-purpose flour
½ tsp baking powder
1 tsp ground allspice
scant ½ cup dried cranberries
½ cup pine nuts, toasted

Preheat the oven to 350°F/180°C. Grease a baking sheet.

Whisk the sugar with the egg until pale and thick enough to leave a trail when the whisk is lifted.

Sift the flour, baking powder, and allspice into the bowl and fold into the mixture. Stir in the cranberries and pine nuts and mix lightly to a smooth dough.

With lightly floured hands, shape the mixture into a long roll, about 11 inches/28 cm long. Press to flatten slightly.

Lift the dough onto the prepared baking sheet and bake in the preheated oven for 20—25 minutes, until golden. Let cool for 3—4 minutes, then cut into ⁵/₈-inch/1.5-cm thick slices and arrange flat on the baking sheet.

Bake the slices for about 10 minutes, until golden. Let cool on a wire rack. When cool, store the biscotti in an airtight container for 2—3 weeks.

Biscotti con arancia ed amarena
Orange and sour cherry biscotti

makes 20–30

1 cup whole blanched
  almonds
1/2 cup dried sour cherries
  or dried cranberries
3/4 cup pine nuts
generous 1 cup all-purpose
  flour, plus extra for dusting
generous 3/4 cup superfine sugar
1 tsp baking powder
1/4 tsp ground nutmeg
1/4 tsp ground cinnamon
zest of 1 orange
2 eggs
2 tsp vanilla extract

Preheat the oven to 350°F/180°C. Line two baking sheets with parchment paper. Roughly chop the almonds and the cherries. Place in a bowl with the whole pine nuts. Mix the flour, sugar, baking powder, nutmeg, cinnamon, and orange zest with the nuts and dried fruit.

Beat the eggs and the vanilla extract together. When combined add the flour mixture and combine to form a firm dough. Turn out the dough onto a lightly floured counter. Knead for 4–5 minutes, or until no longer sticky.

Divide the dough in two, and shape each piece into a long flat log, about 2 inches/5 cm wide. Transfer each log to the prepared baking sheets. Place in the preheated oven and bake for 20–25 minutes, until pale golden brown in color.

Remove from the oven and let cool for 5 minutes. Reduce the oven temperature to 325°F/160°C. Transfer the baked loaves to a cutting board and, using a serrated knife, cut into 1/2-inch/1-cm slices. Arrange the slices flat on the lined baking sheets and return to the oven. Bake for about 15–20 minutes, until dry and crispy. Remove from the oven and let cool. These biscotti can be kept crisp by storing in an airtight container.

Torta di mandorle
Almond cake

Preheat the oven to 325°F/160°C. Generously grease an 8-inch/20-cm round, springform cake pan. Beat the egg yolks with the sugar in a medium-size bowl until pale and thick and the mixture leaves a trail when the whisk is lifted. Stir in the potato flour, almonds, orange rind, and orange juice.

Whisk the egg whites with the salt in another bowl until stiff. Gently fold the whites into the egg yolk mixture.

Pour the mixture into the prepared pan and bake in the preheated oven for 50—60 minutes, until golden and just firm to the touch. Turn out onto a wire rack to cool. Sift over a little confectioners' sugar to decorate before serving.

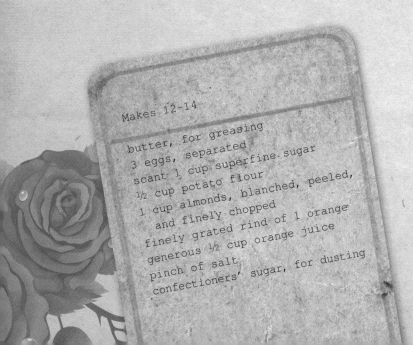

Makes 12-14

butter, for greasing
3 eggs, separated
scant 1 cup superfine sugar
½ cup potato flour
1 cup almonds, blanched, peeled,
    and finely chopped
finely grated rind of 1 orange
generous ½ cup orange juice
pinch of salt
confectioners' sugar, for dusting

Fiorentini
Florentines

Preheat the oven to 350°F/180°C. Grease and flour 2 cookie sheets or line with parchment paper.

Place the butter in a small saucepan and heat gently until melted. Add the sugar, stir until dissolved, then bring the mixture to a boil. Remove from the heat and stir in the golden raisins, cherries, ginger, sunflower seeds, and almonds. Mix well, then beat in the cream.

Place small teaspoons of the fruit-and-nut mixture on the prepared cookie sheets, leaving plenty of space for the mixture to spread. Bake in the preheated oven for 10—12 minutes, or until light golden in color.

Remove from the oven and, while still hot, use a round cookie cutter to pull in the edges to form a perfect circle. Allow to cool and become crisp before removing from the cookie sheets.

Melt most of the chocolate and spread it on a sheet of parchment paper. When the chocolate is on the point of setting, place the cookies flat-side down on the chocolate and let harden completely.

Cut around the cookies and remove from the parchment paper. Spread a little more chocolate on the coated side of the cookies and use a fork to mark waves in the chocolate. Let set. Arrange on a plate with alternate sides facing upward. Keep cool.

makes 40

5 tbsp butter, plus extra for
   greasing, if using
flour, for dusting, if using
⅓ cup superfine sugar
2 tbsp golden raisins or raisins
2 tbsp candied cherries, chopped
2 tbsp preserved ginger,
   chopped
3 tbsp sunflower seeds
¾ cup slivered almonds
2 tbsp heavy cream
6 oz/175 g semisweet chocolate

Acknowledgments

The publisher would like to thank the following for permission to reproduce copyright material:

© Corbis:

8 (bottom, left) Little girl wearing dress

9 (bottom, right) Italian delicatessen storefront

12 (middle, right) Illustration of child dressed in bird of paradise costume

27 (bottom, right) Common Cock Illustration

58 (middle, left) Young girl holding birthday cake

92 (middle, top) Girl hiding under mother's dress

134 (bottom, right) Illustration of child dressed in sparrow costume

134 (middle, left) Two children sitting in surf on beach

142 (middle, left) Father and son sharing watermelon at picnic

169 (middle, right) Adults carrying children on shoulders

176 (top, left) Baking cookies

177 (bottom, right) Many Happy Returns of the Day postcard with St. Bernard

180 (top, left) Red onion layers

180 (bottom, left) Shallots

190 (bottom, left) Illustration of a couple in a canoe

© Getty:

11 (bottom, middle) Basil leaves on white background

Front cover, 32 (top, left) Dried pasta, close-up

Front cover, 92 various forms of pasta

127 (middle, left) Girl (4–5) having breakfast, (B&W)

143 (bottom, left) Family eating outdoors

© Sabine Vonderstein:

10 (bottom, left) Genovia book

26 (left), 102 (middle) striped ribbon

36 (left), 43, (right) 96 (left) green polka-dot ribbon

52 (top, left) Postcard with girl

100–101 Numbers x 10

135 (top, right) Brooch

86–87 (left, right), 128–129 (left, right) pink polka-dot ribbon

© istockphoto.com:

All other incidental images not listed above

© Parragon Books Ltd

All recipe images

Index